Cambridge E

Elements in Politics and Society in East Asia
edited by
Erin Aeran Chung
Johns Hopkins University
Mary Alice Haddad
Wesleyan University
Benjamin L. Read
University of California, Santa Cruz

THE STATE
AND CAPITALISM IN CHINA

Margaret M. Pearson
University of Maryland

Meg Rithmire
Harvard Business School

Kellee S. Tsai
Hong Kong University of Science and Technology

CAMBRIDGE
UNIVERSITY PRESS

Shaftesbury Road, Cambridge CB2 8EA, United Kingdom

One Liberty Plaza, 20th Floor, New York, NY 10006, USA

477 Williamstown Road, Port Melbourne, VIC 3207, Australia

314–321, 3rd Floor, Plot 3, Splendor Forum, Jasola District Centre,
New Delhi – 110025, India

103 Penang Road, #05–06/07, Visioncrest Commercial, Singapore 238467

Cambridge University Press is part of Cambridge University Press & Assessment,
a department of the University of Cambridge.

We share the University's mission to contribute to society through the pursuit of
education, learning and research at the highest international levels of excellence.

www.cambridge.org
Information on this title: www.cambridge.org/9781009356749

DOI: 10.1017/9781009356732

First published 2023

A catalogue record for this publication is available from the British Library.

ISBN 978-1-009-35674-9 Paperback
ISSN 2632-7368 (online)
ISSN 2632-735X (print)

Cambridge University Press & Assessment has no responsibility for the persistence
or accuracy of URLs for external or third-party internet websites referred to in this
publication and does not guarantee that any content on such websites is, or will
remain, accurate or appropriate.

The State and Capitalism in China

Elements in Politics and Society in East Asia

DOI: 10.1017/9781009356732
First published online: May 2023

Margaret M. Pearson
University of Maryland

Meg Rithmire
Harvard Business School

Kellee S. Tsai
Hong Kong University of Science and Technology

Author for correspondence: Kellee S. Tsai, ktsai@ust.hk

Abstract: China's contemporary political economy features an emboldened role for the state as owner and regulator, and with markets expected to act in the service of party-state goals. How has the relationship between the state and different types of firms evolved? This Element situates China's reform-era political economy in comparative analytic perspective with attention to adaptations of its model over time. Just as other types of economies have generated internal dynamics and external reactions that undermine initial arrangements, so too has China's political economy. While China's state has always played a core role in development, prioritization of growth has shifted to a variant of state capitalism best described as "party-state capitalism," which emphasizes risk management and leadership by the Chinese Communist Party (CCP). Rather than reflecting long-held intentions of the CCP, the transition to party-state capitalism emerged from reactions to perceived threats and problems, some domestic and some external. These adaptations are refracted in the contemporary crises of global capitalism. This title is also available as Open Access on Cambridge Core.

Keywords: China, political economy, state capitalism, government-business relations, global capitalism

ISBNs: 9781009356749 (PB), 9781009356732 (OC)
ISSNs: 2632-7368 (online), 2632-735X (print)

Contents

History does not provide such supermarkets in which we can make our choice as we like. Every real economic system constitutes an organic whole. They may contain good and bad features, and more or less in fixed proportions. The choice of system lies only among various 'package deals.' It is not possible to pick out from the different packages the components we like and to exclude what we dislike.

János Kornai (1980: 157)

Forty years of experience of reform and opening tells us: the Chinese Communist Party's leadership is a fundamental feature and the biggest competitive edge of the system of socialism with Chinese characteristics. In military and science and civilian endeavors, in all directions, the Party's leadership is everything.

Xi Jinping (2018a)

Capitalism is not a rigid system. It has evolved and changed over time, shaped by local history, social pressures, and crises ... Markets are not self-creating, self-regulating, self-stabilizing, or self-legitimizing. Hence, every well-functioning market economy relies on non-market institutions to fulfill these roles.

Dani Rodrik and Stefanie Stantcheva (2021: 824)

1 Situating China's Political Economy

Institutional and evolutionary approaches to political economy have established that ostensibly stable systems are pressured to adapt to changing conditions or face the prospect of extinction (Crouch 2005; cf. Greif & Laitin 2004; Nelson & Winter 1982). Postwar capitalism, for example, adopted Keynesian principles of "embedded liberalism" (Ruggie 1982) to ameliorate the damaging societal effects of unfettered markets. Neoliberal reforms during the 1980s subsequently downsized welfare states in many advanced industrial nations facing fiscal crises. Likewise, rapid industrialization in the postwar developmental states of Taiwan and South Korea generated structural changes in government-business and state-labor relations that supported their respective transitions to democracy (Wade 1990). Since its founding in 1949, the People's Republic of China (PRC) has similarly adapted its economic model. In brief, the PRC's model has evolved from emulation of Soviet-style central planning to the early post-Mao era's nonlinear experimentation that combined market reforms and privatization with continued state support of strategic sectors – and under Xi Jinping's rule, resurgence of state intervention through a wide range of mechanisms into core parts of the political economy. Each of these shifts reflects adaptations to perceived opportunities and challenges, some domestic and some external.

Throughout these shifts, social scientists have drawn parallels between China's developmental experience and that of other statist economic models such as mercantilism, the developmental state, and state capitalism. Reform-era China has also been compared with post-socialist countries, large emerging market economies, and advanced industrialized countries. More controversially, some observers have referred to Xi Jinping's rule as "fascism with Chinese characteristics" (Stuttaford 2022; cf. Béja 2019). We situate China's experience in the context of these comparative lenses, with an eye to understanding the depth of such parallels, and the degree to which China's model is *sui generis* historically. In particular, while there are apparent similarities with the East Asian developmental model of Japan, Korea, and Taiwan (Amsden 1992; Haggard 1990; Johnson 1982; Looney 2020; Wade 1990), China's model of political economy diverges notably from these developmental states, and includes qualities associated with predation (Lü 2000; Pempel 2021).

Indeed, China's development has presented puzzles that confound conventional explanations. By tracing the evolution of China's political economy, this Element demonstrates how its idiosyncratic trajectory is not easily explained by existing models. China's empirical departures from the expectations of standard developmental theories have fueled multiple research agendas among scholars of contemporary China and demonstrated the need for conceptual innovation. Notably, as China's political economy has evolved, the distinction between private and state ownership has become increasingly blurred, calling for caution when conceptualizing Chinese phenomena in terms derived from fundamentally different contexts.

Given the expanding role of the Chinese Communist Party (CCP) in the economy since the late 2000s, we observe a shift from a more familiar form of state capitalism to a variant that we call "party-state capitalism." Consistent with an evolutionary and adaptive lens on political economy, we emphasize that China's transition to party-state capitalism is not merely a reflection of Xi Jinping's ascent to the country's top leadership position. Xi's leadership style certainly breaks from that of his reform-era predecessors, as the party-state's responses have become strikingly more mobilizational and coercive, often reflecting his personal preferences. Xi's extreme concentration of authority was reinforced at the 20th Party Congress in late 2022, which violated retirement age and succession planning norms by extending Xi's leadership for a third term and stacking the Standing Committee of the Politburo solely with his acolytes. Nevertheless, as commonplace as it has become to attribute China's turn toward party-state capitalism to "the Xi Jinping effect" (Economy 2018; Esarey 2021; Rudd 2022), we argue that the new model has deep roots in developmental trends and debates that predate his assumption of power. Xi's rise coincided with a series of political and economic challenges in the PRC that emanated from within the country and beyond its borders. As such, we contend that explaining China's political economy under Xi requires understanding how certain policy choices were reactions to challenges that predated his leadership. Attending to the role of endogenous (domestic) and exogenous (international) sources of change demonstrates how China's political-economic evolution resonates with other cases analytically, including political and economic changes in postdevelopmental states, advanced capitalism, and economic securitization during interwar fascism. The CCP's emphasis on regime security has prompted seizure of state control in critical sectors, while other firms (e.g., small and medium enterprises [SMEs], basic services, and manufacturing) remain meaningfully privatized.

Yet efforts to strengthen party control over the economy have presented the CCP with new challenges, both internally and externally. Domestically, we explore the implications of recent conflict in state-business relations, including the party-state's antagonism toward large technology firms and diversified conglomerates. These sectors are sites of the CCP's turn to party-state capitalism, which has been accompanied by the elevation of economic affairs to the level of national security. Driven by concerns over risk management and framed in antitrust rationale, party-state efforts to discipline business actors indicate deepening strains between capital and the state. Internationally, we show that China's new model, which entails blurring of boundaries between state and private actors, has produced a backlash from advanced industrialized countries, where new institutions of investment reviews and export restrictions have begun to reshape global capitalism (Farrell & Newman 2021; Pearson, Rithmire, & Tsai 2022).

Overall, the evolution of China's political economy should be examined in the context of dynamics generated by its model over time in interaction with changes in the national economies that constitute global capitalism. We write at a moment in which capitalist societies throughout the world are reevaluating the relationship between politics and capitalism. This Element contextualizes and compares China's experience in adapting to perceived threats, and also illustrates how China's economic transformation has prompted such a reevaluation in other capitalist contexts.

In this study of political economy, our primary focus is the relationship between the Chinese state and economic actors – primarily firms, owners, investors, and entrepreneurs. Changes in the state-business relationship affect many economic outcomes, including basic indicators such as growth, productivity, and innovation. Because these outcomes are also influenced by factors beyond the state's basic political approach (e.g., the rate of capital investment, global economic conditions, and unpredictable shocks (Kroeber 2016; Lardy 2014, 2019), they are not the focus of this study. Two other topics also are largely outside the scope of this Element. First, we emphasize state-business relations as they are experienced by large firms, particularly those most politically salient to China's government. The shift to party-state capitalism that we observe has had less of an impact on the private small and medium enterprise sector, which is also an important source of growth and employment (Lardy 2014; Naughton 2018; Tsai 2017). Second, scholars have demonstrated the importance of subnational governments in reflecting and adapting policy toward economic actors (e.g., L. Chen 2018; Davidson & Pearson 2022; Eaton 2016; Hsueh 2011; Oi 1999; Pearson 2019; Rithmire 2014; Shen & Tsai 2016; Tan 2021). While local officials play a key role in implementing directives of the central government and promoting their own interests, subnational variation in developmental trajectories remains embedded within the broader context of shifts in China's political economy.

2 Classic Conceptions and Models

This Element's focus on "the state and capitalism" has its foundations in key concepts and theories in political economy. While much of this literature focuses on growth, the features motivating our inquiry are the nature and internal dynamics of China's development, and the evolution of its model over time. One of our central themes is that China's trajectory resonates only partially with conventional understandings of economic development. This section lays out basic ideas and frameworks that are relevant for putting China's political economy, and decades of scholarly analysis of it, into the broadest intellectual context. As general approaches to describing and categorizing political economies, the concepts discussed in the following paragraphs are not equally relevant to China, and none fully captures the country's developmental path and present characteristics. But each provides a comparative analytic lens for understanding China's uniqueness and distinguishing its model and evolution from other patterns.

2.1 Capitalism (versus Socialism)

Capitalism has preoccupied some of the world's most influential philosophers, including Adam Smith, Max Weber, Joseph Schumpeter, and Karl Marx. Although each of these theorists offers a distinctive perspective on the concept of capitalism, including its origins, they share several defining features: capitalism is a modern system of economic organization that leverages transactions based on actors' economic self-interest to increase the productive capacities and developmental outcomes of societies. Smith, Weber, and Schumpeter, again, with some differences, shared a normatively positive view of self-organized economic interests that own and direct capital and other resources without extensive oversight by the state. They emphasized the value of entrepreneurship and innovation as contributing to progress in society, even when it involves – in the words of Schumpeter – "creative destruction."

Marx did not see capitalism as the aggregation of individual interests, but rather, as the expression of class interests. Capitalism's unfolding as a necessary stage of history, to Marx, not only produced unparalleled advances in societies' ability to meet their physical needs (through advancements in the "means of production"), but also sharpened class conflict. These structural contradictions would eventually spark revolution, resulting in a new "communist" society that would end alienation and exploitation. Following Lenin and the Russian revolution, China's communist party revolutionaries hewed to the Marxist critique of exploitative capitalist societies and global imperialism, even though Marx himself emphasized developing the means of production to its "highest stage" prior to overthrowing capitalism. Mao Zedong's revolution of 1949, like Lenin's three decades earlier, emphasized the need for a period of socialism, marked by state ownership, to do the work of capitalism in developing the productive forces. In these classic Marxist conceptions, *private versus state ownership* is the hallmark institution that distinguishes capitalism from socialism.

How production actually happens in economies is the focus of a second conceptual dyad, anchored by market mechanisms at one end and government planning at the other. The concept of "markets" is distinct from capitalism, but bundles naturally with it. For neoclassical economists, markets are the selection mechanism that facilitate market entry and exit through competition (Schumpeter 1911). Mediated by price signals, markets organize horizontal exchange transactions among economic actors – producers, workers, consumers, financiers, etc. At the other end of the spectrum is government planning, whereby political agents such as ministers decide who should produce what for whom and at what cost (Lindblom 1977). Goals of planners may or may not be consistent with productivity and growth, as they may privilege other values related to socioeconomic development or political control. An extreme expression of the state-as-planner model severely limits space for markets. Stalin in the USSR strove to perfect a central planning system, which Mao largely adopted in urban areas throughout the 1950s as a model of industrialization (Brandt and Rawski 2022).

The international economy also features in debates over the relative advantages of markets versus planning. In neoclassical economic visions, a country's ability to leverage its comparative advantage in the international division of labor can be a potent catalyst for growth, beyond what is possible within a national economy. During the 1970s and 1980s, the premier postwar international economic institutions of the International Monetary Fund (IMF),

World Bank, and General Agreement on Tariffs and Trade (GATT, the precursor to the World Trade Organization) envisioned that deeper integration into the international economy was part of the recipe for economic development. Still, in both critical and some neoclassical theories, exposure to international economic forces can be a damaging source of competition and even exploitation (Bhagwati 2004; Evans 1979; Frieden 2006; Lenin 1916). Mercantilist policies deployed by states to protect national economies from these harms include, for example, subsidizing exports and restricting imports, fostering domestic industries, and manipulating payment systems and currencies (e.g., List 1841).

Political economy as an academic field considers not just how economic functions are carried out, but also the role of the state in these systems. While no national economy operates in a void without state influence, the role of the state varies considerably in scope and strength. The most stringent advocates of market capitalism posit the benefits of a severely restricted "night-watchman state," whereby the state's scope is limited "to protecting individual rights, persons and property, and enforcing voluntarily negotiated private contracts" (Buchanan, Tollison, & Tullock 1980: 9) to avoid statist tendencies to crush entrepreneurship and seek rents. Such classic capitalism presumes that markets are largely self-regulating, and that sociopolitical crises arising from capitalism can be fixed primarily by market forces themselves, as well as by technology and productivity advances. Indeed, technological optimists view the continued evolution of technology as sufficient to resolve deep schisms and inequalities catalyzed by advanced capitalism. Disruptions in labor markets and wages would present short-term costs (Chandler 1977).

A middle ground on the appropriate role of the state, albeit still covering a broad spectrum of functions, recognizes the necessity of arm's length regulation by the state to address market failures such as monopoly and environmental degradation. Even the process of liberalization may entail regulation (Vogel 2018). A more activist state may define areas in which market mechanisms dominate and areas in which it takes an assertive role in directing resources, such as in industrial policy. This middle ground is where we find the "varieties of capitalism" literature, which recognizes differences among political as well as market configurations in advanced capitalism (Hall & Soskice 2001). This influential literature stresses a distinction between "liberal market economies" of the Anglo-Saxon capitalist tradition and "coordinated market economies" of the European tradition. While the state maintained a greater posture in the latter compared to the former, steerage by the state was never considered the main driver of growth and development (Thelen 2012), and is not central to these models.

Returning to the distinction between capitalist and socialist systems, János Kornai (2016) identified the distinguishing characteristics of each, listed in Table 1.

Table 1. Primary characteristics of capitalist vs. socialist economic systems

Primary characteristic	Capitalist system	Socialist system
Ruling political group	Ensures dominance of private property and market coordination	Communist party enforces the dominance of public property and bureaucratic coordination
Dominant form of property	Private ownership	State ownership
Dominant form of coordination mechanism	Market coordination	Bureaucratic coordination

Source: Adapted from Kornai (2016: 553).

The preceding discussion lays out stylized, and sometimes idealized, notions of political economy based on classic scholarship. In reality, politico-economic systems are always mixed (Polanyi 1957). Such mixtures are readily identified in the major theoretical approaches that have dominated study of the political economy of development. While recognizing unique aspects of China's developmental model, the most common frameworks invoked for understanding its reform-era experience are theories of modernization, the developmental state, transitions from socialism to capitalism, state capitalism, and to a lesser extent, fascism. We outline each of these theories in the following sections, highlighting their common attention to "getting institutions right" (Rodrik, Subramanian, & Trebbi 2004).

2.2 Modernization Theory

"Modernization theory" encompasses a broad set of ideas originating in the mid-twentieth century that economic and political development progress in tandem and that economic growth generally leads to democratization. Reasoning from a stylized narrative of the Western experience, modernization theorists identified a set of structural changes associated with economic development, including urbanization, education, industrialization, and secularization, which were expected to craft citizens who would progressively prefer property rights and civil rights (Deutsch 1966; Inkeles 1966; Lipset 1959). Sustained growth and the emergence of a politically engaged middle class in particular were posited to generate demand for power sharing, protection of property rights – and, ultimately, multiparty democracy (Almond & Verba 1963; Przeworski & Limongi 1997). Notably, this process was imagined to be universal: any society that experienced economic growth with market mechanisms and private wealth accumulation would undergo social and political changes that lead to democracy.

Modernization theory met significant criticism. Samuel Huntington argued that economic development and social mobilization could destabilize polities and that stronger governments were better equipped than liberal ones to manage the process of modernization (Huntington 1968). Taking a pan-national view, dependency theorists criticized modernization theory for failing to incorporate global or transnational forces; they viewed underdevelopment not as a function of "backwardness" but rather as exploitation or inhibition of the "periphery" by developed "core" countries (Gunder Frank 1966; cf. Dos Santos 1970).

Despite these critiques, earlier expectations that modernization theory could provide insight for China's reform-era development were understandable: many held that as China industrialized through the introduction of markets and a middle class emerged from an urbanized, growing economy, China would embark on a path of political liberalization and, ultimately, democratize. While addressing the prospects for political or regime change in China is beyond the scope of this Element, we note that many Western observers (Gilley 2004; Guthrie 1999; Lardy 1994) and even some in China (Wang 2009) hoped that modernization theory might correctly predict China's developmental trajectory. Reformers in Beijing relaxed socialist-era restrictions on economic activity to allow private-sector development and open the door to international market forces. Decades of spectacular economic growth through industrialization and urbanization ensued.

Yet, clearly, the CCP did not open up to political competition. Instead, space for political contestation has narrowed considerably over time, contravening modernization theory's expectations. A wide range of scholarship on China's middle class and its entrepreneurial class offers explanations for why these groups have not been advocates for political change, including that they have been incorporated into the party-state and that the CCP enjoys broad legitimacy among the public for its achievements (Dickson 2008; Tang 2018; Tsai 2006, 2007; Shi 1997).

2.3 Developmental State

Modernization theory assumes industrialization under relatively laissez-faire conditions rather than specifying the appropriate scope for states in the development process. Its advocacy, generally, of democratic institutions and enabling of society implies that the main drivers for economic development should best come from outside the state, i.e., from relatively autonomous economic actors. It is against this privileging of a more restrained state, as well as alertness to countries' concerns about exploitation through unfettered globalization, that the "developmental state" literature emerged (Woo-Cumings 1999). Successful strategies of developmental states include drawing on their status as "late industrializers" to leapfrog stages of development, especially in the acquisition of critical technologies, and harnessing statist tools to guide the development process (Gerschenkron 1962). Haggard (2018: 10) notes the influence that Gerschenkron had on the developmental state school:

> It is hard to overstate the prescience of the Gerschenkron essay vis-à-vis the subsequent developmental state literature: the most basic idea that industrialization is crucial to catch-up; that development strategies must be seen in an international context; that specialization might be inimical to growth; that technology, increasing returns, and externalities are central features of industrialization; that capitalism is not of a single piece but shows important variation in latecomers; and that institutions – including the state – play crucial roles in the growth process.

The developmental state literature originated out of efforts to explain the unexpectedly rapid industrialization of several East Asian economies. Japan, Taiwan, Korea, and Singapore all managed export-oriented industrialization in the post–World War II period with a set of institutions that did not conform with neoclassical economic norms (World Bank 1993). Technocratic state agents, typically concentrated in specific economic ministries, "picked winners" by identifying and nurturing sectors and firms through industrial policies, including tax breaks and preferential access to credit (Wade 1990). Such targeted state intervention in the economy promoted rather than prevented growth.

The nature of the state – what provides its capacity – in successful developmental models is the hallmark of the theory. The ideal state in important respects approximates a Weberian-style bureaucracy, characterized by meritocratic recruitment and technocratic expertise, corporate coherence, and sufficient autonomy from societal interests to avoid rent-seeking and capture (e.g., Amsden 2001; Johnson 1982, 1995). Countering the implication of earlier works on East Asia that suggested states were depoliticized because they were insulated from society and politics, Evans (1995) emphasizes the relationship between state and society, in particular the degree to which state actors and structures are "embedded" in society. When network ties, especially with the private sector, are dense enough to provide information useful to policy making, the developmental state is more effective. As Doner, Ritchie, and Slater (2005) succinctly put it, developmental states are "organizational complexes in which expert and coherent bureaucratic agencies collaborate with organized private sectors to spur national economic transformation."

China's reform-era experience shares some commonalities with the developmental state, including a late industrializer's sense of urgency to catch up and concomitant prioritization of economic growth through industrial policy. But on balance, China departs from several key features of the developmental state – to the point that we do not find it appropriate to classify it in the same category.

First, compared with the East Asian developmental states, China's economy was relatively decentralized and lacked a "pilot" ministry, like Japan's MITI or Singapore's Economic Planning Board, that directed development in a strategic and holistic manner. Instead, especially in the early decades of reform, China's development was driven by local governments with strong incentives to pursue investment and growth (Breznitz & Murphree 2011; Oi 1999). Scholarship on China's bureaucracy has emphasized the role of meritocracy and promotion incentives (Ang 2016; Lü & Landry 2014; Shih, Adolph, & Liu 2012; Yang 2004), but few, if any, would describe the Chinese bureaucracy as "embedded" or "autonomous." On the contrary, scholarship has emphasized the prevalence of corruption, though scholars differ on whether corruption has been primarily "growth-enhancing" or distorting (Ang 2020; Lü 2000; Rithmire & Chen 2021; Wedeman 2003, 2012).

Second, China retained state ownership, especially over large firms at the "commanding heights" of the economy. Developmental states generated large, vertically integrated conglomerates (the Japanese *keiretsu* or Korean *chaebol*), but state ownership of firms was not significant. Relatedly, while the East Asian developmental states directed credit toward the most productive enterprises, China's state-owned enterprises have had privileged access to subsidized loans from state-owned commercial banks, while the more profitable private sector has faced ongoing barriers in accessing credit.

Third, most developmental states had limited domestic markets and restricted exposure to foreign direct investment (FDI), while China clearly has a large domestic market and FDI featured prominently in its period of high growth. This combination of FDI and a vast domestic market created a highly competitive ecosystem as domestic players upgraded and foreign firms pursued greater efficiency to compete in China's vast middle market (Brandt & Thun 2010).

Fourth, the developmental states were built on anticommunist efforts, lending ruling parties both a mobilizing existential threat (Doner, Ritchie, & Slater 2005) and access to the markets of Western allies. China's economy also eventually grew with access to overseas markets, but, as we go on to discuss, the Chinese bureaucracy was and is that of a Leninist system and organized to facilitate collective production and consumption.

2.4 Post-Socialist Transitions

While the concept of the developmental state refers primarily to late industria-lizers in the postwar period, collapse of the Soviet Union and communist regimes in Eastern and Central Europe led to studies on the political economy of post-socialist transitions. It would not be possible to explain China's evolution without understanding its socialist past, but the gradualism and sequencing of introducing markets and dismantling many aspects of state socialism distinguishes China from post-socialist states in Europe.

Adopting the neoliberal principles of the World Bank and IMF, many post-communist governments implemented radical market reforms ("shock therapy") by privatizing state assets and lifting state controls over prices virtually overnight (Åslund 1995; Weber 2021). The policy logic, as articulated by Jeffrey Sachs, was starkly laissez-faire: "Economic problems solve themselves: markets spring up as soon as central planning bureaucrats leave the field" (Sachs 1993, xiii, cited in Hall & Elliott 1999: 306). However, this was not borne out by Russia and Poland's experiences with the "big bang" approach to reforming socialism. In the immediate aftermath, both suffered extreme inflation, currency devaluation, unemployment, and declines in industrial production – and the intended objective of disempowering existing political and social interests was not achieved, especially in Russia (Murrell 1993).

Furthermore, it became increasingly evident that institutional legacies from the socialist era mediated the reform process, leading to diverse privatization paths and outcomes. Rather than wholesale replacement of planned economy institutions with market forces, East Central European economies exhibited distinct forms of privatization that reflected their particular paths of extrication from state socialism (Stark 1992). By acknowledging sources of continuity and path dependence, this strand of the transition literature provides a more nuanced, nonbinary lens for understanding post-socialist forms of political economy, an insight that resonates with our observations about China's hybrid model.

Comparative studies of post-communist systems generally contrasted the Soviet Union's painful exit from socialism from China's more experimental and gradualist reform approach (Szelenyi & Mihályi 2020). Yet economists also engaged in internal debate over explanations for China's rapid growth. Was it due to unscripted experimentation with incremental reforms or due to liberalization, internationalization, and privatization (McMillan & Naughton 1992; Sachs & Woo 1994; Woo 1999)? As discussed in Section 3, these mechanisms are not mutually exclusive in practice, but accounts that discount the role of the central and local states in China's reform process are incomplete.

Over time, others observed constraints to deeper reform following state capture by early beneficiaries of reform in transitional economies (Frye 2010; Hellman, Jones, & Kaufman 2003). This is a somewhat counterintuitive finding given that conventional interest-based analyses would expect the short-term losers of reform (e.g., laid-off workers, former managers, pensioners, etc.) to present a greater obstacle to further marketization. Instead, many post-communist transitions have been suspended in a "partial reform trap" due to opposition from newly enriched owners of privatized assets (Hellman 1998). Political dominance of early reform winners thus obstructs full transition to a market economy. China has similarly faced challenges in liberalizing some economic sectors due to resistance from vested interests and associated venality (Pei 2006). A key difference from the European post-socialist cases, however, is that China's reform-era leadership has never embraced the teleological agenda of transition from state socialism to market capitalism. Unlike the post-socialist transition economies that liberalized following the collapse of their ruling communist parties, the CCP continues to monopolize political power in China and, as discussed next, state ownership or control of strategic economic sectors persists.

2.5 State Capitalism

The frameworks discussed thus far derived from particular historical and regional experiences with development – modernization theory described the path of advanced industrialized democracies; the developmental state explained rapid growth in East Asia's newly industrialized countries; and the post-socialist transitions literature focused on the former Soviet Union, Eastern and Central Europe. By contrast, the concept of "state capitalism" has been used to describe a wider swath of political economies, both geographically and historically. State capitalism spans contexts as diverse as wartime Germany, the Soviet Union under Lenin and Stalin, Nasser's Egypt, and contemporary large emerging market economies such as Brazil, India, and Indonesia. Writers at both ends of the left-right ideological spectrum have used the term pejoratively. "State capitalism" was first articulated in 1896 by Wilhelm Liebknecht, a founder of the Social Democratic Party of Germany (SPD), at the Second International Congress (Sperber 2019, 104). In response to misperceptions that the SPD advocated state socialism, Liebknecht retorted, "Nobody has combatted State Socialism more than we German Socialists, nobody has shown more distinctively than I, that State Socialism is really State Capitalism!" (Liebknecht 1896, 4). This antistatist sentiment was echoed during the 1950s when Marxists in the US critiqued Stalinism as "state capitalist" for extracting surplus value from labor in an exploitative manner akin to private capitalism (James, Dunayevskaya, & Boggs 1950).

Half a century later, the term "state capitalism" experienced a revival. After the 2008 global financial crisis, neoliberal critics of state interventionism in the economy repopularized the term to describe countries with state-owned enterprises (SOEs), national oil companies, and sovereign wealth funds (Bremmer 2010). In this encompassing definition, democratic countries such as Brazil, India, Indonesia, and Norway are also regarded as state capitalist. State capitalism conveys a more derogatory connotation, however, when referring to autocracies such as China, Russia, Iran, and Saudi Arabia, with some preferring the term "authoritarian capitalism" (Bloom 2016; Carney 2018; Chen 2022; Huang & Tsai 2022; Witt & Redding 2014) or "autocratic capitalism" (Kornai 2016) to underscore regime type.

Bracketing its normative connotations and diverse historical pedigree, political economists have analyzed state capitalism as a categorical alternative to the varieties of capitalism literature that focused on Western market economies (Hall and Soskice 2001). In the study of comparative capitalism, state capitalism broadly denotes mixed economies in which the state retains a dominant role amidst the presence of markets and privately owned firms. Contemporary scholars have converged on a general definition that highlights the centrality of a capacious and autonomous state in steering economic development through not only targeted ownership stakes but also a suite of other institutional and financial interventions (e.g., Kurlantzick 2016; Musacchio & Lazzarini 2014; McNally 2012; Naughton & Tsai 2015). Tools – again, not wholly unique to state capitalism – include preferential access to credit, subsidies, industrial policy guidance, and control over managerial personnel. State influence in the economy is exercised selectively, and typically concentrated in strategic sectors, such as defense, energy, communications, and finance.

Because state economic intervention occurs in both the developmental state and state capitalism, it is worth distinguishing between them to clarify their definitional boundaries. A general similarity is that both types of political economy entail indicative planning and policies to support select sectors. A second observation is that both concepts are agnostic about regime type even if they are more often associated with authoritarian variants. Some, but not all, developmental states in Asia transitioned from autocratic to democratic rule over time; and as indicated previously, state capitalist economies span all regime types. Yet the two models differ in important aspects, starting with the centrality of state ownership and management of strategic sectors typical to state capitalism. Based on this key distinction, we would not regard postwar Japan and Korea as state capitalist due to private-sector dominance of their leading industries, while Singapore can be regarded as both a developmental state and state capitalist due to the prominence of its government-linked cor-porations and sovereign wealth funds.[1] State capitalism also envisions a wider range of tools for direct and indirect state control of firms through appointment of SOE executives, state-owned asset management companies, and equity stakes in private businesses.

Section 4 elaborates on how China has evolved from a more familiar form of state capitalism to "party-state capitalism," such that earlier developmental goals have been overshadowed by an abiding focus on political power and risk management.

2.6 Fascism

In Section 4, we describe the evolution of China's state capitalism into its more politically focused, party-state directed version, which we call party-state capit-alism. This evolution recalls earlier theoretical debates about shifts in models. During World War II, German social scientist Friedrich Pollock's (1941) essay, "State Capitalism: Its Possibilities and Limitations," inspired a strand of debate that seeded the Frankfurt School of critical theory (Gangl 2016). Identifying "state capitalism" as the historical successor to "private capitalism," Pollock (1941: 96) differentiated between democratic and totalitarian variants, and described the latter as follows:

> Under a totalitarian form of state capitalism, the state is the power instrument of a new ruling group, which has resulted from the merger of the most powerful vested interests, the top-ranking personnel in industrial and business manage-ment, the higher strata of the state bureaucracy (including the military); and the leading figures of the party's victorious bureaucracy. Everybody who does not belong to this group is the mere object of domination.

Deliberating in the context of trends in continental Europe's political economy, founding members of the Institute for Social Research associated the erosion of "monopoly capitalism" with the politicization of economic relations (Sperber 2019). Herbert Marcuse (1942) contended that the modern state was conceived to be separate from society, "*non*-political and subjected to its own laws and standards" (p. 70). Under National Socialism in Germany, however, Marcuse observed elimination of the "rational division of functions between the state and society" (p. 71), such that "economic expansion must not only be supplemented, but superseded by political expansion and domination" (p. 74). The result was fascism.

---

[1] Of the four postwar East Asian developmental states, Taiwan had a relatively higher proportion of SOEs, but they generated less than 17 percent of the GDP at their peak level in the early 1970s and underwent privatization in the late 1980s.

Fascist regimes are characterized by the centrality, even totality, of the state as a political solution to perceived economic and political crises. Citing Japan and Germany's early-twentieth-century experience with "revolution from above," Barrington Moore (1966) identified a fascist (capitalist reactionary) path to modernity in contrast to bourgeois revolutions that led to democracy and peasant revolutions that led to communism. As a reactionary, ultranationalistic mode of development, fascism is most commonly associated with the Italian and German movements that seized power amidst dual crises of capitalism and liberal democracy (Berman 2019). Popular dissatisfaction with national disunity, stagnation in economic and technological modernization, and a desire to elevate the nation's international status produced "almighty states" seeking to dominate "every sphere of life," assuming "responsibility for the collective life of the population and the economy, which in turn had to serve national goals" (Berend 2006: 99). Given the complexity of defining fascism (Griffin 1991; Paxton 2004), here we engage fascism as an "historical event," rather than as a designation of regimes, and focus on the fascist treatment of the economy (Berezin 2019: 356).

Operationally, fascism's economic dirigisme privileged the political goals of states above individual or group interests, including those of private capitalists. However, fascist regimes never sought to eliminate private property rights, but rather, to direct the efforts of capitalists:

> Although entrepreneurs had independence on investing, decisions about products, research and development and other fields of company management, the state set strict limits, regulating prices and distribution and influencing and often ordering investment decisions. Important goals of the state bureaucracy were realized by state-owned companies and the compulsory cooperation between state-owned and private firms. (Berend 2006: 109)

The "primacy of politics" in the fascist stance toward capitalists was exemplified in interwar Germany and Italy. Both states not only vowed to protect private property and promote economic growth, but also sought to create "a system in which the state's 'needs' and 'goals' were not threatened by unregulated markets and 'selfish' capitalists" (Berman 2009: 571).

Logistically, fascist economic dirigisme involved corporatist relationships, a drive for national self-sufficiency justified by the perceived threat of foreign control over critical inputs, and "growing confusion between the roles of private enterprise and the state" (Lyttelton 1973 141). State ownership existed alongside private ownership, even oligarchy, because the state could exert control through its political prerogative. *Control*, rather than ownership, was paramount. Therefore, capitalism and private property were formally embraced, but "willingness to assert the power of the state vis-à-vis the market ... represented a real solution to the problems of the modern liberal capitalist order" (Berman 2009: 571).

China's transition from state socialism to party-state capitalism differs markedly from the European and Japanese paths to fascism. Fascist movements explicitly opposed socialism, while the contemporary CCP remains a Leninist political party that embraces socialist values in official discourse, while maintaining a mixed economy with extensive private ownership. Another key difference, as we will show, is that party-state capitalism in China emerged in the process of reforming market socialism rather than as a movement built on the ruins of failed political and economic models. Unlike interwar fascism, party-state capitalism does not entail ideological or institutional rejection of what came before. We return to this comparative theme at the end of the Element after delineating the core features of China's political economy as they have evolved over time.

3 Evolution of China's Political Economy

China's developmental path differs from those of developmental states significantly, starting from the fact that the country's turn to markets began atop its experience with state socialism. After grasping political control in 1949, the CCP gradually but definitively nationalized ownership of the means of production as a series of campaigns in the 1950s persuaded or forced business owners to turn their assets over to the state (Hinton 1968; Solinger 1987). From the mid-to-late 1950s through the onset of reforms in 1978, urban China was organized around work units (*danwei* 单位), in which economic enterprises owned by various levels of the state also constituted the link between Chinese citizens and state services, social welfare, and expectations of political behavior (Walder 1986). To be sure, not all urbanites enjoyed equal access to the state's largesse (Perry & Li 1997) and not all elements of capitalist consumption or behavior were eliminated (Solinger 1987; Zhang & Liu 2019), but overall, political and social life in Maoist China was organized around collective consumption and production.

In rural China, land reforms in the late 1940s and early 1950s first eliminated private land ownership, and organized peasants into agricultural production units consisting of twenty-five to fifty families charged with meeting production targets. In 1956, those production units were turned into collectives comprising hundreds of families. During the Great Leap Forward (1958–61), collectives became even larger communes amid a drive to overtake the UK in steel production. Political radicalism, manifest in, for example, excessive grain procurement and "backyard furnaces," along with weather conditions, combined to cause a famine that killed tens of millions of rural Chinese (Dikotter 2010; Yang 1996).

3.1 The Era of Reform: Experimentation and Gradualism

The dual cataclysms of the Great Leap and Cultural Revolution (1966–76) offered an aperture for substantial political and economic changes upon Mao's death in 1976. Deng Xiaoping's assumption of power in 1978 marked the beginning of the "reform and opening" (*gaige kaifang* 改革开放) era, during which the CCP introduced markets in rural and urban China in a manner that was gradual and experimental; did not dismantle the core institutions of state socialism; and retained a commitment to the CCP's own monopoly on political power. These reforms prompted a fundamental reorganization of the factors of production, in particular unleashing labor productivity as many rural dwellers were allowed to migrate to cities for new opportunities.

In the rural sector, reforms began in Anhui and Sichuan, the inland provinces most affected by the Great Leap famine (Kelliher 1992; Yang 1996). The Household Responsibility System, which became national policy in the late 1970s and early 1980s, permitted plots of collectively-owned land to be leased to households. Markets were layered on top of state procurement quotas; whatever households produced in excess of quotas could be sold on markets. By all accounts, agricultural productivity accelerated, accumulating rural savings that in turn financed industrialization. Land in rural China would remain owned by collectives, and the household registration (*hukou* 户口) system, which assigned each Chinese citizen a place of residence and designated them "agricultural" or "nonagricultural" (urban), linked rural citizens to collectives and prevented them from formally migrating to cities as it had done since the early PRC period.

Rural industrialization through "township and village enterprises" (TVEs) was a primary engine of economic growth in the 1980s and early 1990s. Legally owned by local governments, TVEs surprised policymakers and observers alike in their astonishing rates of growth and productivity; their output grew at an average annual rate of 30 percent during the 1980s. While a significant number of TVEs were actually privately owned firms masquerading as a more politically acceptable corporate form – a phenomenon known as "wearing the red hat" (*dai hong maozi* 戴红帽子) – most were owned by local governments. The unexpected productivity of these public enterprises has been attributed to tax-sharing arrangements between levels of the state in China during the reform period. Early-1980s fiscal reforms allowed local levels of government to control revenues generated in their jurisdictions, creating incentives for local governments to run "their firms as diversified corporations, redistributing profits and risks, and thereby allowing the rapid growth of rural industry with limited resources" (Oi 1999:12; Solinger 1984; Whiting 2001).

In urban areas, experimental and gradual reforms to state-owned enterprises met with less success than rural reforms (Naughton 2006). Despite introducing dual-track pricing and incentive pay for well-performing managers, SOEs continued to lag in productivity, resulting in significant nonperforming loan problems for state banks (Lardy 1998). It was not until the late 1990s that significant numbers of SOEs underwent corporate restructuring and privatization (Lin 2017). Most of the economic growth in urban areas during the first two decades of reform came from the private sector and foreign investment, sometimes in combination.

Unlike the developmental states in East Asia, where private industry benefited from various preferential policies, in the first few decades of China's reform era, the private sector had a liminal status. Lacking in formal political protections, petty capitalists were subject to lingering ideological suspicion and episodes of political crackdown (Kraus 1991). Nonetheless, local governments depended on their economic contributions and were incentivized to support local entrepreneurs by both fiscal systems (retaining tax revenue) and the party-state's organizational management system (cadre responsibility contracts that conditioned bonuses and promotion on meeting critical state goals, economic growth chief among them) (Ang 2016; Edin 2003; Oi 1999; Whiting 2001). In this context, capitalists relied on adaptive informal institutions, widely practicing "informal coping strategies devised . . . to evade the restrictions of formal institutions" (Tsai 2006: 117).

Private entrepreneurs, for example, were essentially excluded from the state-run banking system, and therefore developed a creative range of informal financing mechanisms to support their businesses (Tsai 2002). Other strategies, such as disguising private ownership through different corporate forms, facilitated private-sector growth in the gaps between formal institutions and informal encouragement to pursue economic development. Partially because the overall approach to reform in China was experimental and gradual, over time widespread adoption of these informal practices produced endogenous change in formal political institutions, including the legalization of private enterprises (with more than eight employees) in 1988 and the 2001 decision to allow private entrepreneurs to join the CCP itself.

The opening to global capital was similarly experimental and gradual, allowing the CCP to assess and contain its effects while managing internal dissent over opening to the world (Pearson 1992). Four coastal Special Economic

Zones were designated in 1979, and fourteen coastal cities were opened by the mid-1980s. The piecemeal introduction of foreign capital and competition enabled the CCP to assess the economic and political effects of global capital. Politically, the sequencing of reform and opening contributed to the regime's ability to reframe its embrace of global capital and market reforms by creating initial "winners" of reform (Shirk 1993). The regime benefited from the growth effects of foreign capital before it initiated more politically and socially costly economic reforms, reframing a narrative of class struggle into one of national competition in an age of globalized markets (Gallagher 2005).

China's accession to the World Trade Organization (WTO) in 2001 catalyzed a phase of deepening global integration by which the country became the "world's factory." Between 2001 and the onset of the global financial crisis in 2008–09, China became the world's leading exporter, comprising 10 percent of world exports by 2011 (WTO 2002). China's current account surplus surged from a little over 1 percent of GDP in 2001 to 10.1 percent at its peak in 2008 (IMF 2012). Over the same period, FDI grew from around $40 billion to $186 billion, and the People's Bank of China (PBOC) accumulated vast foreign exchange reserves, exceeding $2 trillion by 2010, which it invested largely in US treasury bonds.

Economically, foreign investment brought new technology and management knowhow into China, nurturing an emergent class of domestic business elites and firms that would grow into competitors (Pearson 1992). China combined large volumes of FDI with an enormous domestic market, and Chinese firms upgraded as foreign competitors localized production to reduce costs. At the same time, Chinese firms improved quality to compete for the vast middle market (Brandt & Thun 2010). China's labor supply and the promise of its market size attracted FDI, but Chinese firms also proved innovative in manufacturing and technology commercialization (Nahm & Steinfeld 2014). Undoubtedly, government policies at multiple levels facilitated these benefits of globalization, including joint venture requirements, investments in research and development, and controversially, requirements for technology transfer as well as mimicry and outright intellectual property theft (L. Chen 2018; Bresnitz & Murphee 2011). Many local and sectoral protectionist efforts were the product of decentralized and fragmented politics (Tan 2021) as well as the preferences of many within the CCP to retain state control over strategic sectors (Hsueh 2011).

Significant restructuring of state-owned enterprises, entailing laying off millions of workers and dismantling the "iron rice bowl" of cradle-to-grave social welfare enjoyed by urban state sector workers, occurred during the late 1990s. Around 85 percent of local government-owned industrial firms underwent corporate restructuring between 1997 and 2003 in a strategy called "grasping the big, releasing the small" (*zhuada fangxiao* 抓大放小) enterprises (Zeng & Tsai 2011: 40). The process was politically thorny, involving ideological contestation over ownership. Plagued by behaviors such as asset stripping, de facto privatization of state-owned enterprises led to widespread discontent and stagnation in less dynamic regions that were the heart of Mao-era industrialization (Hurst 2009; Lin 2017; Shue 1988).

3.2 "State Capitalism" and the Limits to Market Liberalization

Embracing the private sector, restructuring state-owned firms, and opening to the global economy diminished and reshaped the role of the state in China's political economy, but major forms of state intervention and state ownership were retained. Most fundamentally, state-owned firms persisted into the twenty-first century and, especially for those owned by the central government in Beijing, many expanded and became vastly more powerful in the 2000s. As central SOEs underwent restructuring, their ownership was transferred from various ministries and concentrated in the State-owned Asset Supervision and Administration Commission (SASAC) by 2003. Over the next several years, many behemoth SOEs would undergo initial public offerings (IPOs) on stock exchanges in China and abroad, a policy intended to introduce discipline and modernize corporate governance while retaining state financial control. For its part, SASAC was designed to "financialize" the state's role in governing SOEs to enhance their competitiveness (Wang 2015; Naughton & Tsai 2015).

Preserved state ownership at the commanding heights of the economy and in globalized or strategic sectors, such as shipping, telecom, natural resources, and aviation, broadly conformed with the main features of "state capitalism," and China's political economy was described as such (Bremmer 2010; Lin & Milhaupt 2013; Naughton & Tsai 2015). But the state's economic role was not limited to ownership of firms. The basic institutions governing inputs to production – land, labor, and capital – coalesced around state control, even as the regime experimented with market mechanisms and undertook reform (Looney & Rithmire 2017). In land, decades of reforms nonetheless left local governments as owners of "state-owned" land and the only actors who could convert rural, collectively owned land into urban land for construction. Local governments increasingly relied on land-lease revenues to meet budgetary expenditures, and contrary to the expectations of modernization theory, urbanization was described as "state-led" rather than driven primarily by markets and migration (Hsing 2010; Ong 2014).

In the financial system, state-owned banks continued to dominate, offering low deposit rates for China's vast household savers, and capital controls kept savings domestic. This combination of institutions, a version of what economists call "financial repression," gave policymakers access to a large pool of capital (Lardy 2008). Bank credit continued to be subsidized and readily available to SOEs and, increasingly, local government borrowers (Liu, Oi, & Zhang 2022), but also found its way to the private sector in greater volumes. On the labor front, the household registration system underwent piecemeal reforms while the state retained basic control over population movements, and therefore the labor supply and demands for social and political inclusion in China's cities (Wallace 2014; Solinger 1999).

In addition to state ownership and control over major factors, policymakers pursued broad guidance over the country's developmental direction. The National Development and Reform Commission (NDRC), built amid the reform of the State Planning Commission, did not plan production and consumption as a conventional state planner would, but did mobilize resources and direct policy toward both national developmental goals and regional efforts in the 2000s. Regionally, campaigns directed investment to specific parts of China left behind by globalized coastal areas, such as "Opening the West" (*xibu da kaifa* 西部大开发, 2000), "Revive the Northeast" (*zhenxing dongbei* 振兴东北, 2003), and "The Rise of the Center" (*zhongbu jueqi* 中部崛起, 2004). Substantive concerns about the country's specialization in low value-added industries and dependence on foreign technology began to coalesce in 2006. A new drive for "indigenous innovation," manifest in the Medium- and Long-Term Plan (MLP) 2006–20, targeted increased spending on research and development, reduced dependence on foreign technology, and increased productivity-driven growth. Barry Naughton suggested that the MLP heralded the revival of industrial policy in China (2021: 49), but nonetheless notes that firms remained the primary actors until the global financial crisis provided a turning point for economic policy and political contestation over China's future.

4 A New Model: Party-State Capitalism

By the late 2000s, China faced a critical juncture in its reform process as the global financial crisis called into question the sustainability of its export-dependent model and decades of double-digit growth.[2] State capitalist measures to ameliorate the effects of the crisis, combined with rising social instability and rampant corruption, called for policy responses. Domestic debate over the future of reforms ensued. Intellectuals associated with the "New Left" sought

---

[2] Portions of this section appeared in Pearson, Rithmire, & Tsai (2021).

correctives to what they perceived as the more pernicious effects of markets and private ownership, especially inequality, bourgeois decadence, and a reduced role for the state (Li 2010). Similar views on the need to undo the harms of Chinese capitalism underlay the "Chongqing Model" of Bo Xilai, party secretary of the megacity Chongqing (Huang 2011). Bo's vision was often contrasted with the neoliberal "Guangdong Model" advocated by provincial party secretary for Guangdong Province, Wang Yang. In Chongqing, reforms under and preceding Bo Xilai entailed massive state investment in infrastructure, urbanization, public works projects, and political mobilization, notably the "smash black" anticorruption campaign and the "singing red" Maoist nostalgia movement. By contrast, in Guangdong, Wang Yang touted liberalization, "small government," and public accountability to redress the problems of capitalism in China, especially corruption (Rithmire 2012). This elite and public debate about China's direction of reform ended in scandal, with Bo's expulsion from the CCP immediately preceding the 18th Party Congress, at which Xi ascended to the role of paramount leader.

When Xi Jinping assumed power in 2012, it seemed plausible that the PRC's fifth generation of leadership might introduce bolder market reforms to break through bureaucratic and business interests vested in preserving a "partial reform equilibrium" (Hellman 1998). Initially, Xi's administration indeed stated that "markets should be the decisive force in allocating resources," and took up efforts at what he called "supply side reforms," or structural reforms in arenas such as tax collection and financial liberalization (Rosen 2021; Xinhua 2013). But these reforms either stalled or generated economic instability, as in the case of equity market turmoil (discussed in Section 5). Instead of market reforms, Xi indicated that China needed to adjust its economic model to a "new normal" of more modest growth, and under his leadership the CCP has extended its authority and reach – organizationally, financially, and politically – into China's domestic and foreign economic relations. While prior developmental goals remain relevant, they have been overshadowed by initiatives that place politics in command, with state economic interventions more directly in the service of the party's political survival. Moreover, privileging the party's monopoly of power in the contemporary period has brought about substantive changes in the party-state's role that are not fully captured by existing concepts, and constitute a more *sui generis* form of political economy: party-state capitalism.

This section examines three sites at which we can observe the manifestation of party-state power, all of which extend beyond familiar forms of economic dirigisme. First, the tools of managing China's economy entail not only state ownership and market interventions, but increasing institutional encroachment in additional realms of domestic economic activity. These new modalities of control, including financialization and emboldened roles for the party in corporate governance, empower new agents and prioritize discipline and monitoring by party-state actors. Second, while depictions of state capitalism typically suggest a zero-sum relationship between the state and private firms, we document a mixing and blending of ownership, function, and even interests. Conceptual dyads in the study of political economy – state versus capital, public versus private ownership – have long been problematic in the study of post-Mao China and continue to lose meaning. In particular, although the ownership category of firms remains of interest to observers, in China the distinction between state and private ownership is increasingly blurred in practice. Third, the political imperative driving party-state capitalism is affecting the behavior of global firms and organizations that have stakes in China's market. The state has shifted from courting foreign capital with preferential treatment during the initial decades of reform to expecting that not just domestic firms but also multinationals and their home governments, respect political red lines drawn by the CCP. Taken together, the emergence of party-state capitalism has been accompanied by "securitization" of China's political economy, such that economic affairs are increasingly regarded as national security issues. This securitization, in turn, has strained China's relations with wealthy countries (loosely those part of the Organization for Economic Co-operation and Development, or OECD) and fomented suspicion of Chinese firms operating abroad, a phenomenon detailed in Section 5.

4.1 Party-state Encroachment

The first site at which we can distinguish China's party-state capitalism is institutional expansion of the state's role in the economy beyond public ownership of large enterprises in strategic industries. Standard definitions of state capitalism referenced previously do not capture the range of tools deployed by the Chinese state. Especially notable is the emergence of institutional and financial modes of party-state encroachment into the private sector.

4.1.1 Expansion of Party Cells

A basic indicator of the Chinese party-state's institutional expansion is the resurgence of party cells inside enterprises, including private businesses and even foreign firms. The presence of party cells in private and other "non-state" organizations in itself is not new.[3] Since 1925, the CCP Constitution has

---

[3] The term "non-state" in this context can be read as "private." Chinese official sources use the category "non-state" (*fei guoyou*), which covers small and large private firms, as well as Sino-foreign joint ventures. We use the term private except where referencing Chinese official statistics and statements.

specified that any entity with more than three party members should have a party unit (Hou 2019), though in practice, party cells in private enterprises and foreign-invested enterprises have varied in their levels of activity and relevance (Koss 2021; Pearson 1992; Yan & Huang 2017). Under Xi Jinping, emboldening party control and party building in firms became a key priority (Leutert 2018), as laid out in numerous party and SASAC declarations. For example, a 2013 party circular stated that an SOE's party unit had to be involved in important decisions of the firm, specifying not just important personnel matters but also development and operational strategies, mergers, and acquisitions (Zhang 2019, 58). At the 19th Party Congress, Xi (2017) declared that the "Party exercises overall leadership over all areas in every part of the country."[4] The next year, the securities regulator promulgated rules mandating the establishment of a party unit in domestically listed firms, and required companies to provide the "necessary conditions" for party activities to occur (CSRC 2018). Both domestic and international observers have noted the enhanced vigor of party organizations in private firms and joint ventures (Wong & Dou 2017; Yan & Huang 2017). The CCP (2018) itself reports that by the end of 2017, 1.88 million nonstate firms had established party cells, accounting for over 73 percent of all nonstate firms. The government has suggested that party units within firms are supplemental and helpful, and even frequently welcomed. According to the State Council Information Office in 2017, "Most investors welcome and support the Party organisations to carry out activities inside their enterprises" (quoted in Blanchette 2019: 1). Conversely, many business owners have reportedly expressed anxiety about the potential for state intervention in the management of firm affairs via party organizations (Hou 2019). International investors echoed this concern, as seen in a German industry federation's warning that party interference could lead to a retreat of international firms (He 2017). Blanchette (2019) suggests that the private sector was not singled out, and that this move merely reflected the party's broader efforts to "have insight and input into *all* economic, civil, and political activity within the country." As yet, however, the degree of party intervention in actual firm decisions is difficult to discern and disentangle from the effects of other trends in the economy.

4.1.2 Politically Motivated State Shareholding and "Financialization"

A second distinguishing characteristic of party-state capitalism in China is the expansion of state capital well beyond firms that are majority-owned by the state, a process scholars describe as "financialization of the state" (Guthrie,

---

[4] Fewsmith (2018: 18) concurs that "Xi has asserted the primacy of the party, inserting 'the party controls everything' into the party constitution for the first time."

Xiao, & Wang 2015; Naughton 2019; Wang 2015). Since 2003, the party-state has institutionalized its ownership of firms in SASAC, a body that appoints managers and generally acts like a "capitalist asset manager" rather than a classic state owner (Guthrie, Xiao, & Wang 2015: 76; Sutherland & Ning 2015). While financialization of the state's role in managing SOEs has been well documented, the role of state capital *outside* majority ownership, including in so-called "mixed ownership" firms discussed in Section 4.2.1, is a more recent development, but nonetheless widespread and politically consequential.

Since 2012, the CCP has encouraged the establishment of "state-owned capital investment companies" that would "invest in non-state-owned enterprises in various ways" to advance industrial policy goals and provide capital to nonstate firms with "strong growth potential" (PRC State Council 2013, 2015). The funds were also expected to generate investment returns in important sectors of the national economy (Naughton 2019a). Investments generally took the form of state shareholding firms acquiring small (typically less than 3 percent) minority stakes in nonstate firms through purchases on equity markets. This practice exploded during the stock market crisis of summer 2015 when selloffs suddenly erased the gains of the prior year in the Shanghai and Shenzhen Stock Exchanges. As part of a menu of bailout actions, the China Securities Regulatory Commission arranged for a "National Team" of state shareholding funds to purchase over 1.3 trillion RMB of stocks on both exchanges between June and September, eventually holding half the shares of all listed firms (Chen, Zheng, & Liu 2020). This broad financial intervention was not about allocating capital toward growth ends, but rather about *risk management* and *maintaining stability*, core components of the CCP's narrative about political control.

Expansion of state shareholding has not only been adopted in emergencies. Starting in 2013, the CCP began exploring the idea of "special management shares" for media and technology companies – firms with strategic and political importance. Special management shares are a class of equity shares with higher voting rights or special governance power per share (Fang & Wang 2017). The first purchase under this scheme occurred in 2016, when the *People's Daily* acquired one percent of a Beijing-based internet company and installed a "special director" on the board who possesses veto power over ideological content (Guo 2017). In 2021, the China Internet Investment Fund, comanaged by the Cyberspace Administration of China and the Ministry of Finance, purchased one percent equity stakes in ByteDance (owner of TikTok) and Weibo (similar to Twitter), respectively, and were granted one director seat on each of their boards (Zhai 2021). These one percent equity stakes carry a disproportionately high degree of political influence over tech firms, which were subject to a series of regulatory crackdowns in 2020–22 (Collier 2021).

4.1.3 Industrial Policy's Extended Reach

Another manifestation of the party-state's economic activism is evolution in the scope of industrial policy. Industrial policy has long been a feature of the Chinese reform-era economy (Heilmann & Shih 2013; Naughton 2019b). Its intensified use as a policy tool since the mid-2000s – and its extension under Xi Jinping to the private sector – is evident in the ambitious *Made in China 2025* strategic plan. Launched in 2015 to encourage indigenous innovation, technological self-reliance, and industrial upgrading, the broad contours of the initiative resonate with traditional "state capitalism." The scope of Made in China 2025 also is not new, but rather evolved directly from two earlier initiatives: the Medium- and Long-Term Program for Science and Technology Development, launched in 2006, and the Strategic Emerging Industries initiative of 2010. But its implementation, more than previous industrial policies, involves private firms as both the targets and executors (PRC Ministry of Industry and Information Technology 2017). Private firms are executors in the sense that the CCP expects them, rather than just SOEs, to be the innovators and global competitors. They are targets in that they are not expected to achieve a high level of innovation and global competitiveness without the state's help. The policy entails large-scale mobilization of capital through government "industrial guidance funds," managed by both state and private capital managers, and targeted toward private firms with innovative capacity in critical sectors.[5]

The semiconductor sector is instructive. The national government and many local levels of government established semiconductor investment funds beginning in 2014. The first stage of the national fund alone allocated $21 billion for the sector, which combined with local government contributions, reached $77 billion (Zhao 2021). Established in 2019, the second stage of the fund allocated $30.5 billion and is expected to raise twice the amount of the initial fund (Zhao 2021). In many cases, the funds themselves are run by private managers, including private equity firms who take government-supplied capital and raise additional funds from private sources to comprise the fund (Rithmire & Li 2019). An OECD (2019: 48) report observes significant support for firms at nearly every part of the domestic semiconductor supply chain, and finds that most of these firms "do not conform to China's own definition of an SOE," complicating international understandings of ownership and influence in the

---

[5] The "state-owned capital operation companies" are often major investors in the industrial guidance funds (Naughton 2019). By mid-2018, there were 1,171 government guidance funds with an investment target of 5.85 trillion RMB, equivalent to nearly seven percent of China's total GDP that year (Economic Daily 2018).

industry. Combined with alarm at China's drive for technological self-sufficiency, this blurring of ownership has deepened international confusion and generated political backlash against Chinese businesses abroad.

These forms of institutional encroachment by the party-state beyond ownership (firm-level party building and the proliferation of state capital) are consistent with a narrative about China's political economy that sees an emboldened state. However, these new developments complicate the state's role in the economy in ways that go beyond those in the state capitalism paradigm. As such, the actual impact of state investment on the private sector should be analyzed in a nuanced manner. On the one hand, the government's stated rationale for extending investments into private firms is that many deserving firms lack sufficient access to credit, especially as regulators have cracked down on informal finance and shadow banking in recent years (Hachem 2018, Tsai 2017). Research on minority state shareholding in other national contexts suggests that state investment can aid rather than supplant the private sector (Inoue, Lazzarini, & Musacchio 2013). On the other hand, political motivations underlie the flow of state investment to certain firms. The official rationale for special management shares in internet firms is, "to do a good job of controlling and promoting the scientific development of internet companies. This requires the establishment of a reasonable method of supervision through [corporate] governance" (Guo 2017). In addition to picking winners through state shareholding, the party-state is adopting new means of monitoring private enterprises.

4.2 Blending Functions and Interests of the State and Private Sectors

China's private sector has been a major source of the country's economic "miracle" and outpaced the contributions of the state-owned sector by most measures (Lardy 2019). A common description of the private sector's economic value is "60/70/80/90," meaning that private firms contribute to 60 percent of China's GDP and generate 70 percent of innovation, 80 percent of urban employment, and 90 percent of new employment (Zitelmann 2019). Meanwhile, SOEs continue to accrue losses and suffer declines in productivity. To some degree these problems are endemic to the sectors in which state enterprises have been concentrated historically – strategic and declining industries – but that explanation is secondary to insufficient profit-maximizing behavior and misallocation of capital by financial institutions (Lardy 2019). Despite the importance of the private sector to China's economy, the common connotation of the term "private" – that it is relatively hived off from the state – is belied by features of ownership and function. We explore here the intensifying blending of not just ownership but also function and interests, in a manner that compromises the familiar public/ private conceptual binary and illustrates the distinctive political logic of party-state capitalism.

4.2.1 Fuzzy Ownership and Control

Ambiguity surrounding the definition of private ownership in China calls into question a sharp distinction between state-owned and private firms. The Company Law of the People's Republic of China defines with relative clarity the different types of state-owned enterprises, such as limited liability and joint stock companies.[6] By contrast, the law does not directly define "private" (nonstate or *minying* 民营) holdings. Rather than being characterized by a delineated bundle of rights in which the private owner is defined as the residual claimant of assets and income and the bearer of risks, subject to government taxation and regulation, in China the term "private" is mainly a residual legal category (Oi & Walder 1999).[7] Moreover, in vernacular terms, the "private sector" itself includes enterprises with diverse origins, financing, and corporate governance structures. Businesses founded by private entrepreneurs de novo or in partnership with foreign investors differ meaningfully from those restructured from the public sector through asset stripping and insider privatization (Ding 2000; Huang 2008; Lin 2017). Although both indigenous private enterprises and privatized SOEs reside in the same ownership category in nomenclature, their shareholders possess varying degrees of autonomy from the state in practice.

Complicating this landscape is the advent of "mixed ownership," which the party-state has promoted actively since 2013. The parameters of mixed ownership, like private ownership, have not been defined clearly or consistently (Naughton 2019a: 179).[8] The party's Third Plenum Central Committee meeting in 2013 called for rapid implementation of mixed ownership, defined as "cross

---

[6] State-owned enterprises include traditional state-owned enterprises and state assets that have been corporatized as limited liability companies or shareholding limited companies (Lardy 2019: 19). A significant subset has listed shares on stock markets in China or abroad, i.e., are shareholding companies in which the state is the majority, or dominant owner (Lardy 2014: 47–48). Such companies can be linked to the central state or to subnational jurisdictions such as provinces, municipalities and counties.

[7] See also The Property Law of the PRC (2007: ch. 5). On the underdevelopment of legal institutions for the private sector, see Nee and Opper (2012), and Segal (2003: 41). The few laws governing private enterprises cover, for example, registration, the number of owners, and so on (Garnaut et al. 2012, ch. 10). Even the otherwise highly specific 2020 Civil Code, Part 2 Subpart II of which discusses property ownership, does little to delineate what constitutes "private" property (NPC 2020).

[8] "Mixed ownership" was proposed as early as 1999, at the 4th Plenum of the 15th Party Congress (Decision 1999).

holding by, and mutual fusion between, state-owned capital, collective capital, and non-public capital" (Chinese Communist Party 2014). It allows private capital to acquire minority stakes in SOEs and may be viewed as "partial privatization" with the goal of making state capital more efficient (Economy 2018: 112–14; Meyer & Wu 2014). It also allows SOEs and state funds to take ownership shares in private enterprises. By mid-2017, SASAC reported that mixed ownership had been introduced to over two-thirds of all central state-owned firms (Lardy 2019: 91). However, evidence is limited that the injection of private capital into less efficient state firms is achieving the claimed effects of alleviating the financial burden of state banks that extend credit to SOEs or enhancing the productivity of those firms. A 2014 survey of private business leaders at the Bo'ao Forum ("the Asian Davos") revealed anxiety that SOE representation, even as minority owners, would effectively allow SOE members to gain control of corporate boards (Meyer & Wu 2014). Indeed, a more political interpretation of mixed ownership is that "it provides a way for the state to direct private capital to serve national development and political priorities" (Xie 2017).

The mixed ownership and other financialization strategies discussed here deepen longstanding ambiguities surrounding the definition, parameters, and position of private ownership in China. In particular, these party-state strategies – and there is little doubt they are driven by the CCP – highlight the porous distinction between ownership and control. Indeed, it seems as though the PRC government now values *control* over ownership, or at least has decided that ownership is not a necessary condition for state control. Although in all systems state control is exercised through means other than ownership, such as regulation and legislation, these strategies provide avenues of potential state influence directly into firms themselves. The ultimate impact on firms' performance, measured by growth, innovation, and so on, is as yet unclear (Huang & Véron 2022; Zhang 2019).

These old and new sources of ambiguity around ownership and its connection to control of firms keep private economic actors in abeyance, neither secure enough in their autonomy from the state to pursue their own interests with ease, nor necessarily able to benefit from the state's largesse or legitimacy. Ambiguity has been a central feature of the CCP in reform, at times facilitating creative action on the part of state and societal actors (Segal 2003; Tsai 2002), and other times emboldening the state to repress actions perceived as threatening (Stern & Hassid 2012). The political logic of sustained ambiguity in ownership is to tether economic actors to the state and limit their scope for independent action, all with the motivating principle of mitigating risk to the party-state itself.

4.2.2 Governance Functions of Private Firms

Meanwhile, private firms have become key actors in supporting the state's domestic security objectives. Maintenance of social stability has been a political priority for the CCP, particularly since 1989 (Wang & Minzner 2015). The digital revolution, however, has diversified China's security industry, as seen in the party-state's growing reliance on technology-intensive surveillance tools and big data to monitor and discipline its large population (Xiao 2019; Xu 2021). In both instances, private firms overwhelmingly dominate the supply of hardware, technology, and information that comprise China's expansive surveillance apparatus (Huang & Tsai 2022). Conventional notions of state capitalism would expect a sector as critical and strategic as domestic security to be dominated by subsidized public entities. Instead, China's largest video surveillance producers, Hikvision and Dahua, were founded by private entrepreneurs. The two firms have ranked among the top five publicly listed security companies globally since 2015 – and of particular interest, public units constitute the bulk of their sales. The relationship between China's surveillance equipment companies and the party-state is reminiscent of the military-industrial complex in the US, except in this case, the products are geared toward maintaining domestic rather than national security. Private businesses are developing technologically sophisticated products to satisfy the party-state's vast demand for public surveillance equipment (cf. Weiss 2014) and profiting from this demand in the process (Huang & Tsai 2022).

Relatedly, a digital-era addition to China's monitoring regime is its emerging "social credit system" (Xiao 2019; Tsai, Wang, & Lin 2021). Initiated in 2014, the system seeks to create a synthetic assessment of "creditworthiness" and "trustworthiness" for individuals and businesses by aggregating digital data on their social and economic activities. The latter goes beyond traditional financial indicators of credit history, extending to normatively "sociable" or "unsociable" behaviors such as donating blood, jaywalking, time spent playing video games, and "spreading rumors" on social media. Those with higher social credit scores enjoy discounts on purchases, priority admissions to schools for children, and lower interest rates on loans. Punitive measures include public shaming, inability to book train/plane tickets, more expensive health insurance premiums, suspension from social media accounts, and so forth. Whether the scores are used for commercial purposes or more Orwellian scenarios, the initiative relies on the capabilities and cooperation of private firms (Liang, Kostyuk, & Hussain 2018).

Thus far, the relationship between private technology companies and different branches of the party-state is multifaceted – at times competitive, and yet increasingly mutually dependent. In 2015 the People's Bank of China selected eight private technology companies to pilot consumer credit scoring. Three years later, however, the bank tried to curtail Alibaba and Tencent's independent social credit programs due to concerns about their potential to market risky financial products (Hornby, Ju, & Lucas 2018). Nonetheless, both companies have developed social credit scoring systems, drawing on the digital data of their users as well as that provided by various government entities. In addition to accessing the records of Alipay's one billion users, Sesame Credit collects judicial rulings from the court system and blacklists those who have been convicted.[9] In effect, Alipay assists in enforcing court decisions about imposing "credit sanctions" by downgrading the Sesame Credit score of convicted debtors or suspending their Alipay accounts altogether (PRC Supreme People's Court Network 2015).

After the outbreak of Covid-19 in 2020, individual health and travel data became integrated with Alipay and WeChat's digital payment platforms. Both developed a Health Code app that assigns a traffic light color (green, yellow, or red) to indicate the risk level of each user based on one's recent travel history and purchases (e.g., cold medicine). The health codes were not only used for government-sponsored contact tracing of Covid-19 cases, but also became required for entry to stores, restaurants, office buildings, public transportation, residential complexes, schools, etc. throughout the pandemic. Public health surveillance through these private sector platforms became normalized in local governance (Liang 2020). Despite – or perhaps because of – Alipay's vast trove of Chinese citizens' data, the party-state reined in its owner, Ant Group. Citing antitrust concerns and risks to consumers, in November 2020 Beijing abruptly blocked Ant's $39 billion IPO and forced it to undergo restructuring that would separate Alipay from its credit card and consumer loan businesses.

Concurrently, private firms in China have assumed state functions to achieve other policy goals. Large internet companies embraced the Xi administration's poverty alleviation efforts in ways that surpassed the expectations of standard corporate social responsibility programs and are not contracted for by the government in standard outsourcing schemes. In this sense, we observe a merging between party-state and private enterprises in achieving public goals. Alibaba, for example, deployed its Taobao e-commerce platform (akin to eBay) to develop rural product markets and connect rural villages. To be sure, extending e-commerce to rural markets represents a business opportunity, but success

---

[9] As of mid-2019, China's courts had identified 14.43 million "dishonest persons" and their blacklisting has prevented 26.2 million airline ticket purchases and 5.96 million train tickets (Wang & Lan 2019). The identities of "dishonest persons" are listed in a public database maintained by the PRC Supreme People's Court at http://zxgk.court.gov.cn/xgl/.

in doing so has involved Alibaba in a variety of noncorporate roles, including funding rural road construction, partnerships with local authorities in creating e-commerce training programs for cadres and villagers, and more (Li, A. 2017). Country Garden, one of China's largest real estate developers, has supported modernization of the practices of agricultural cooperatives, even sending "poverty alleviation cadres" to live in villages to earn villagers' trust and understand their needs, methods similar to those of poverty alleviation "work teams" dispatched by the party-state itself (Xue 2017; cf. Perry 2019). The reproduction of Mao-era mass line discourse and tactics by the vanguard of China's capitalists – property developers – provides further evidence of the blurring public-private divide that once animated fierce political struggle, and even revolution.

Research on the role of large internet platforms goes further in conceptualizing these "private" firms as complements to the state. Liu and Weingast (2018) view Taobao, the online trading platform owned by Alibaba, as developing a "modern legal system that enforces contracts, resolves disputes, and prevents fraud." They further argue that the "government has off-loaded a substantial part of the development of law to private actors." Given that these private actors lack juridical authority to enforce their own "laws," an alternative interpretation of the emergence of such a parallel legal system is that China's private internet companies themselves have joined with the state in a way that also creates hospitable conditions for their capital accumulation. Beijing never directly "off-loaded" developing the rule of law – or surveillance, or poverty alleviation, for that matter – to the private sector. Contract enforcement, social stability, and rural development are all public goods that private entrepreneurs value for both normative and instrumental reasons. In the context of China's largest SOEs, Lin and Milhaupt (2013) observe that their managerial elites have assembled "what Mancur Olson (1982) called an 'encompassing organization' – a coalition whose members 'own so much of the society that they have an important incentive to be actively concerned about how productive it is.'" China's private technology companies constitute such encompassing organizations as well. Their size and social reach explain why they appear to partner with the party-state to manage Chinese society and also why the party-state seeks direct oversight of their activities.

4.3 Expecting Extraterritorial Political Adherence

A third site at which to observe party-state capitalism in contemporary China, one that has not yet received scholarly attention, is the expectation of party-defined political correctness not just by domestic economic actors, but also foreign corporations that do business in China and in territories over which it claims sovereignty. Some firms were proactive in demonstrating political compliance by establishing party cells in their China offices. Since 2017, however, a growing number of major foreign brands and organizations have been pressured to express contrition for various political faux pas, primarily relating to how Hong Kong, Taiwan, and Tibet are portrayed in their advertisements, websites, or social media (Niewenhuis 2019). Table 2 provides a nonexhaustive list of such apologies by prominent multinationals.

This heightened political sensitivity marks a distinct change from the 1990s and 2000s when Chinese localities competed with one another to attract foreign direct investment (FDI) by offering a host of concessionary policies, such as tax breaks, preferential access to land and credit, and lax oversight of labor and environmental practices (Zweig 2002). China's openness to FDI differentiates it from the East Asian developmental states at comparable phases of industrialization (Kroeber 2016; Liu & Tsai 2021). Although foreign investors have faced their share of challenges in China, these frustrations were more regulatory, cultural, and operational than political in nature. As a result, China has been the developing world's leading recipient of FDI since 1991 and attracted the most FDI globally between 2002 and 2006 (UNCTAD, various years).

Intensified political monitoring and censuring of foreign capital is a more recent expression of party-state capitalism. For several decades, Beijing's objections to comments and events perceived to challenge its sovereignty/ territorial claims were largely directed at national governments and institutions that hosted controversial figures such as the Dalai Lama or leaders from Taiwan. Since the mid-2010s, however, the party-state has progressively extended its political radar to multinational corporations (MNCs). In addition to publicized solicitation of formal apologies by foreign capital, businesses with significant stakes in the China market have adjusted their discourse and behavior, whether due to direct pressure or self-censorship. When a general manager of a US National Basketball Association (NBA) team tweeted support for Hong Kong protesters in 2019, the league was extensively criticized by China's state-owned China Central TV, which suspended its NBA broadcasts and stated, "[W]e think any remarks that challenge national sovereignty and social stability are outside the category of freedom of speech" (Shih 2019).[10] When protests erupted in Hong Kong against a proposed extradition bill with China in 2019, Cathay Pacific Airlines suspended staff who participated in or expressed social media

---

[10] The NBA subsequently became proactive in keeping its players from offending China. In 2022, the Houston Rockets dismissed a player who was an outspoken critic of human rights abuses in China (Thiessen 2022).

Table 2. Multinationals pressured by China to apologize for "political errors"

Company	Date of apology	Political error
Audi	3/15/17	Used map of China without Taiwan and parts of Tibet and Xinjiang
Muji	10/2017	Map in catalogue did not include Senkaku Islands
Delta Air Lines	1/12/18	Listed Taiwan and Tibet as countries on website
Zara	1/12/18	Listed Taiwan as a country on website
Marriott Int'l	1/12/18	Listed Tibet, Hong Kong, and Taiwan as countries on customer survey
Medtronic	1/15/18	Listed Republic of China (Taiwan) as country on website
Mercedes-Benz	2/6/18	Quoted Dalai Lama on Instagram
Gap, Inc.	5/14/18	T-shirt with map of China did not include Taiwan
American Airlines	6/25/18	Listed Taipei under Taiwan as a country on website
United Airlines	6/25/18	Listed Taiwan as country on website
McDonalds	1/19/19	TV ad in Taiwan showed student ID with Taiwan as a country
UBS	6/13/19	Economist Paul Donovan referred to a "Chinese pig" during audio briefing
Versace	8/10/19	T-shirt with "Hong Kong" did not list "China" after it
Givenchy	8/12/19	T-shirt with "Hong Kong" did not list "China" after it; "Taiwan" listed after "Taipei"
ASICS	8/12/19	Listed Hong Kong and Taiwan as countries on website
Coach	8/12/19	Listed Hong Kong and Taiwan as regions separate from China on website, T-shirt with "Hong Kong" without country following it, and "Taiwan" listed after "Taipei"
Calvin Klein	8/13/19	Listed Hong Kong and Taiwan as separate countries or regions on website
Valentino	8/13/19	Listed Hong Kong and Taiwan as separate regions on website
Swarovski	8/13/19	Listed Hong Kong as country on website
NBA	10/6/19	Houston Rockets General Manager Daryl Morey tweeted support for protesters in Hong Kong

Table 2. (cont.)

Company	Date of apology	Political error
Tiffany & Co.	10/7/19	Showed advertisement with model Sun Feifei covering one eye (Hong Kong protest reference)
Apple	10/9/19	Hosted app HKMap.live used by protesters in Hong Kong to track police
Dior	10/17/19	Delivered presentation in China showing map without Taiwan
Burger King	3/20/20	Burger King Taiwan referred to "the Wuhan pneumonia" on social media
Nature Journal	4/9/20	Associated origin of Covid-19 virus with Wuhan and China
HSBC	6/4/20	CEO did not immediately sign petition organized by CCP's United Front Work Department supporting new National Security Law for Hong Kong
Adidas, Burberry, H&M, Lacoste, Nike, etc.	2021	Members of Coalition to End Forced Labour in the Uyghur Region boycotted cotton from Xinjiang
JPMorgan Chase	11/24/21	CEO Jamie Dimon joked that JPMorgan will outlast the CCP during visit to Hong Kong during the centennial year of both institutions

Sources: T. Chen (2018); Dawkins (2019); Jiang (2019); Kinder (2021); McArdle (2020); Niewenhuis (2019); Prasso (2020); Sevastopulo (2021).

support for the demonstrations, followed by the resignation of its CEO (Freed 2019). When China introduced a National Security Law for Hong Kong the following year, nearly all of the territory's tycoons and international business leaders signed a statement organized by the party's United Front Work Department in support of the law *before* its text was even released (Prasso 2020). News outlets refusing to retract their choice of words or coverage of sensitive topics (e.g., *New York Times*, *Wall Street Journal*, and *Washington Post*) have seen their reporters expelled from China on short notice (Stevenson 2020; Tracy, Wong, & Jakes 2020). Political correctness on the part of foreign capital figures in state capitalism, but it is expected under party-state capitalism.

4.4 From State Capitalism to Party-State Capitalism

Table 3 summarizes the main differences between state capitalism, as it emerged in the post-Mao era, and party-state capitalism as it has taken form since the late 2000s. As indicated in the "State Capitalism" column of Table 3, Chinese state capitalism from early on already contained features – notably party cells and party-controlled appointment of SOE managers – not widely found in other state capitalist systems.

The novel manifestations of party-state capitalism outlined previously – enhanced party monitoring and industrial policy, deepening ambiguity between the state and private sectors, and growing political assertiveness with foreign capital – suggest considerable infrastructural power on the part of the party-state (Mann 1984). Indeed, most accounts of state capitalism in China emphasize attempts to preserve control over economic actors, as does our analysis of party-state capitalism. Yet it is important to recognize, and pursue research about, how the state is constrained in executing its strategic intentions, including by negative externalities of party-state capitalism itself. Principally, the earlier era of state capitalism in China was characterized by a rough alignment of interests among the state, local officials, and firms who all pursued economic growth and, frequently, personal prosperity (Ang 2020, Dickson 2008; Wedeman 2012). In the context of China's growing global economic footprint and emphasis on regime security, party-state capitalism may threaten this alignment of interests, complicating implementation of economic policy and producing conflict between private firms and the state. In what follows, we identify two sources of constraints on state power – domestic state-business relations (Section 4.5) and China's global engagements (Section 6.1).

4.5 Influence of Big Business under Party-State Capitalism

Charles Lindblom (1977) observed that all governments depend on economic actors to provide jobs, growth, innovation, and other things that states value. While Lindblom focused on the power of firms in democratic market systems, this insight also applies to state capitalist systems, even in the context of a Leninist regime focused on the party-state's centrality. "Reciprocal dependence" (Culpepper 2015) underlies state-business relations in contemporary China: the state still relies heavily on nonstate investment and economic activity by firms and business elites who wield significant power. We noted one such example of the state's dependence on business in our discussion of Alibaba and Taobao. This reciprocal dependence, which from the point of view of political control by Beijing is a longstanding principal-agent problem, has been well

Table 3. From state capitalism to party-state capitalism in China

	State capitalism (late 1990s to late 2000s)	*Party-state capitalism (since late 2000s)*
Core motivation	Protect core state assets to create wealth and protect interests at home and abroad	Enhanced CCP monitoring and control to ensure political survival
State ownership and financial stakes	SOEs concentrated in strategic sectors SASAC as asset manager	Financialization of the state via state-owned capital investment companies, and state purchase of special management shares in private media and tech companies
Private sector	Ambiguity in definition of nonstate (*minying* 民营) enterprises Private firms operate with relative autonomy and instrumentally in pursuit of profits	Blurring of ownership categories including rise of "mixed ownership enterprises" Private firms in strategic sectors regarded as tools of party-state's goals Private conglomerates and tech giants scrutinized for risk
Party branches	Primarily in SOEs and large private firms	Extension of party cells to over two-thirds of all nonstate firms Installation of "special directors" in tech firms, e.g., to veto media content
Industrial policy	Targeted at SOEs and mid-tier industrial sectors Preferential access to credit and subsidies	Industrial guidance funds in critical sectors, and targeting the private sector for implementation (e.g., Made in China 2025, military-civil fusion)
Moral hazard	Soft budget constraint of SOEs	Prioritization of stability begets state receivership for troubled firms New layers of agents beyond Party's disciplinary systems
Management[11]	Top management of SOEs appointed by CCP Top executive positions (general manager, party secretary, board chair) held by different people Latent party cells	Heightened inspections, rotations, and punishment of management via anticorruption campaigns Increased joint appointments of top executive positions (e.g., party secretary and board chair) More prominent role of party cells in corporate governance
Foreign economic policy	"Going out" investment led by SOEs	Belt and Road Initiative Political correctness expected by MNCs

Source: Drafted by authors.

---

[11] Summarized from Leutert (2018).

documented in the study of Chinese politics (e.g., Cai 2014, Li & O'Brien 1999; Lin 2017; Tan 2020). Under party-state capitalism new agents, created especially through financialization mechanisms, reside outside of that system and dissipate the party-state's personnel control. The majority of capital in the new industrial guidance funds is sourced and managed at the provincial and municipal levels, or by nonstate actors (Naughton 2019a). China Minsheng Investment Group is a prime example. Founded in 2014 by over 50 private companies that invested $75 billion (China Minsheng Investment Group n.d.), Prime Minister Li Keqiang gave it the imprimatur to be "the Morgan Stanley of China" and invest in strategic sectors. Bad management and outright corruption ensued. Within five years, China Minsheng accrued over $45 billion of debt and had to be rescued by the PRC State Council (Chen & Rithmire 2020).

Another situation in which we observe this structural power of firms is when their activities seem to conflict with the party-state's prioritization of stability and focus on risk mitigation, frequently ensnaring the state in the financial problems of even nonstate firms. Overly indebted, large private companies have been described as "grey rhinos" that pose systemic risk to the country's banking system (Almanac of China's Banking and Finance 2017; Gao 2020). By virtue of their size, complexity, and potential disruptive power, these firms constrain the state's autonomy and exist in what Lowi called "a state of permanent receivership" (Lowi 1979). Anbang Insurance Group, for example, was nationalized in 2018 following trophy acquisitions that included the Waldorf Astoria Hotel (Hancock 2018). Other huge private firms, such as HNA Group (owner of Hainan Airlines), have similarly been censured for acting recklessly abroad. Concern about these threats to China's financial health and international image have pressured Beijing to discipline such conglomerates and assume responsibility for their excesses.

Like other "state capitalist" and indeed capitalist political economies, China has its share of extraordinarily wealthy individuals and powerful firms, both of whom can threaten the state and limit its autonomy. Regardless of whether oligarchs accrue their wealth through party-state connections or not, they have strong incentives to defend that wealth (Winters 2011), a practice that frequently conflicts with the policy goals of the party-state itself. For example, several pilot programs to tax residential real estate have failed over the years despite potential benefits for state revenues. In addition to threatening the material interests of real estate developers and their local government allies, such a property tax would require officials to declare their assets (Cho & Choi 2014).

Lastly, we recognize that Chinese companies – whether state or private, at home or overseas – may successfully cultivate state actors to work on their behalf. Arthur Kroeber (2016: 104) cites a phrase popular among Chinese citizens and officials: "There are no state-owned enterprises, only an enterprise-owned state." Although this depiction may be exaggerated, we concur with the underlying insight: just because the state has a large role in the economy does not eliminate the possibility that business interests may capture elements of the policy-making and implementation process. Indeed, the report that over 95 percent of "officially defined large private companies" have CCP connections indicates a measure of mutual dependence and vulnerability (Yan & Huang 2017: 38, nt. 7). While this Element emphasizes the extension of state capitalism into party-state capitalism, various forms of "capital" retain the driving logic of capital – its accumulation.

5 Explaining the Shifting Model

We are not the first to identify a marked change in China's political-economic model. The resurgence of the state in China's economy and society has featured prominently in social science accounts, especially since the rise of Xi (Lardy 2019; Minzner 2018). While treatments of Chinese politics in a number of arenas have focused on Xi's initiatives (e.g., Li 2017), we find that sources of endogenous and exogenous change were present before his ascent, and that still other pressures presented themselves early in his tenure. We do not view the shift to party-state capitalism as a manifestation of long-held intentions of the CCP or simply as a reflection of an idiosyncratic and powerful leader, but rather as a series of self-reinforcing reactions to perceived threats and problems (cf. Leutert & Eaton 2021). We locate endogenous and exogenous origins of these threats.

5.1 Endogenous Sources of Change

In identifying endogenous sources of change, we find that China's political-economic institutions and practices generated dynamics that the CCP viewed as posing potential threats to its monopoly on political power and, therefore, requiring resolution. Macroeconomically, as discussed in Section 3, the Chinese economy post-WTO accession relied excessively on external demand for growth, while Chinese exports were generally concentrated in lower value-added sections of industrial supply chains. Chinese policymakers had emphasized the importance of enhancing domestic demand since at least the Asian Financial Crisis in the late 1990s. The issue of macroeconomic imbalances took on greater urgency after the 2008 Global Financial Crisis, which exposed the fragility of global demand and was framed in party-state discourse as a "new normal" of less rapid but more internally driven growth (Holbig 2018). Yet the response to the crisis itself created problematic economic dynamics. China's large stimulus was conveyed only partially through fiscal spending and the rest in imperatives to state banks to lend. The vast majority of credit went to SOEs and to local governments and into real estate development and infrastructure construction. The ballooning debt of both the private and public sector eventually produced alarm about the systemic risks posed by large debt burdens (Liu, Oi, & Zhang 2022; Rithmire 2022).

Corruption, and the associated fear of attenuated party discipline, was another endogenous source of threat. China's reform era involved an embrace of capitalist development through what scholars have called "special deals" (Bai, Hsieh, & Song 2019) or "profit sharing" (Ang 2016) primarily between local officials and firms. These relationships were mutually beneficial and involved forms of corruption – namely, bribery, whether through basic kickbacks or the kind of socializing typified by discussions of "*guanxi* 关系" – that facilitated commerce and growth. By the late 2000s, however, corruption seemed to present a challenge to the CCP's legitimacy and capacity to govern effectively (Pei 2016; Wedeman 2012). That Xi's first major political initiative was a historic anticorruption campaign indicates his concern about the issue.

Meanwhile, Xi's early years in power were marred by financial instability, especially the stock market crisis that began in 2015. To bolster confidence in equity markets and allocate capital to nonstate actors, policymakers touted the Shenzhen and Shanghai exchanges starting in 2014, inspiring waves of IPOs and expanding investment, chiefly by retail investors (as opposed to institutional investors). The rapid expansion of equity capital ended in an even more rapid selloff that began in the summer of 2015, during which the Shanghai index fell about 18 percent from its peak and Shenzhen's dropped by over 30 percent in a matter of weeks. The collapse accelerated in part because of widespread margin lending and online peer-to-peer (P2P) lending platforms, many of which were beyond the state's regulatory reach and whose activities surprised authorities who did not anticipate or understand them (He and Li 2020). After briefly showing signs it would tolerate a "market correction," the state quickly intervened to arrest the collapse in asset prices by deploying a National Team of funds to inject nearly 3 trillion RMB into the exchanges, holding shares of half of all listed firms at the peak (Li, Zheng, & Liu 2022). At the same time, regulatory authorities suspended IPOs and launched investigations into journalists and market participants for "spreading rumors" or facilitating excessive margin lending. The state's response to the financial crisis – first embracing market forces and then stepping in to stymie their impacts – demonstrates the risk management logic of asserting party-state control.

5.2 Exogenous Sources of Change

A series of events occurring outside China's borders constituted exogenous sources of perceived threat to the CCP and its economic model. More generally, the Color Revolutions in Eastern Europe and Central Asia and the mass movements associated with the Arab Spring were viewed as cautionary tales within the CCP. This perception was reinforced by civil unrest in Tibet (2008) and Xinjiang (2009), events that would eventually beget a massive expansion and deployment of the state's coercive apparatus in those regions, including internment camps for Uyghurs in Xinjiang that have attracted the designation of "genocide" (Greitens, Lee, & Yazici 2020).

While these political events produced a general threat mentality, external events in the economic realm contributed more directly to shifts in the political economy. Whistleblower Edward Snowden revealed that the US had deployed a cyberweapon against Iran and that the National Security Agency (NSA) had breached the servers of Huawei by inserting a "back door" into hardware used by the telecommunications giant. These revelations amplified voices within China saying that reliance on foreign technology poses a threat to national economic advancement and security. Within a few years, new laws and policies, especially the massive industrial policy campaign Made in China 2025 (announced in 2015), would frame technological advancement in terms of national security and existential threat.

Clearly, based on this timeline, dating the shift to party-state capitalism is more complex than identifying a single shock or temporally compressed set of decisions. Such is the nature of change in economic models. Even when single exogenous shocks are hypothesized to spur significant transformation, for example the oil shocks of the early 1970s (Gourevitch 1986), the rise of the knowledge economy in the 1990s (Hall 2020), or the Covid-19 pandemic (McNamara & Newman 2020), they produce diverse aftershocks as they are refracted through various domestic institutions, histories, and sociopolitical processes. Moreover, the timeline shows that many of the more acute threats occurred after Xi's term began, especially the Snowden revelations, the

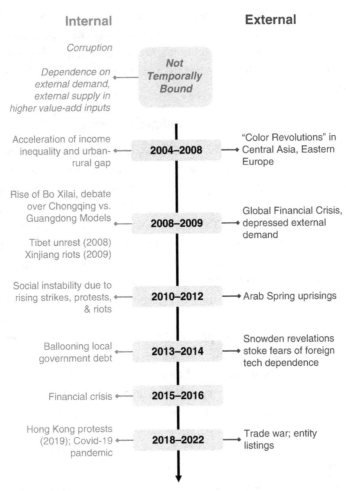

Figure 1. Perceived internal and external threats since the mid-2000s

financial crisis in domestic equity markets, and the emergence of a global pandemic from within China's borders. We emphasize the contingency inherent to the increasing reliance on the party-state itself to remediate problems in China's political economy. Party-state capitalism, much like China's earlier reforms, does not reflect the execution of a longterm masterplan, at least before Xi's rise to power. Rather, the totality of perceived threats to the party-state and challenges of managing problems of economic reforms led policymakers to rely on instruments of party control and technologies of party governance (e.g., campaigns) that then reinforced the party-state's power and centrality within the economy.

5.3 Legal and Developmental Securitization

The party-state's anxiety over perceived internal and external threats has resulted in increasing securitization of China's political economy (Pearson, Rithmire, & Tsai 2022). Since the mid-2010s, a steady progression of laws relating to national security have been enacted that require compliance by Chinese firms, especially those in the technology sector (see Table 4). The encompassing 2015 National Security Law stipulates that economic security (Article 19) and financial stability (Article 20) constitute national security concerns that should be protected by the state (People's Republic of China [PRC] 2015). The 2017 National Intelligence Law (People's Republic of China [PRC] 2017) further requires "firms, individuals and other organizations" to "cooperate in national intelligence work and keep confidential the [information] that it or he knows" (Article 7). Other laws – concerning counterespionage, counterterrorism, cybersecurity, antiforeign sanctions, and data security – similarly compel firms to support the party-state's security efforts and share relevant data and information.

These laws directly complement China's "military-civil fusion" developmental strategy, jointly introduced in the 13th Five-Year Special Plan by the CCP, State Council, and Party's Central Military Commission in 2015. The military-civil fusion initiative seeks to engage private businesses in achieving national defense objectives by encouraging cooperation between commercial and military technology efforts in research and development. Coupled with the Made in China 2025 industrial policy, and as echoed in the 14th Five-Year Plan (2021–25), Beijing's prioritization of indigenous innovation to reduce dependence on foreign technology reveals not only a sense of insecurity about the country's level of technology, but also proactive efforts to engage private firms in contributing to national priorities. The state recognizes that private tech firms are better poised than SOEs to develop frontier technology in artificial intelligence, 5G, biotech, aerospace, and electric vehicles. Multilayered laws and initiatives have developed under party-state capitalism to ensure that enterprises in these areas operate in the interest of national security even as they are driven by commercial motives. Combined with the rise of party-state capitalism, this securitization of China's political economy has stoked counterreactions from OECD countries and contributed to changed dynamics in global capitalism. Section 6 elaborates on these recent trends.

Table 4. Laws ascribing national security roles to Chinese firms

Name	Year	Notable clauses
Counterespionage Law	2014	Citizens and organizations shall facilitate and provide other assistance to counter-espionage efforts (Article 4). The state protects and rewards those who make major contributions to this effort (Article 7).
National Security Law	2015	Establishes "economic security" and "financial stability" as pillars of national security (Articles 19, 20). Enterprises, among other organizations, have responsibility and obligation to preserve national security (Article 11), and shall cooperate as required by national security efforts (Article 78).
Counter-Terrorism Law	2015	Telecommunications operators and internet service providers shall provide technical interfaces, decryption, and other technical support assistance to state organs conducting prevention and investigation of terrorist activities (Article 18).
Cybersecurity Law	2016	Network operators shall protect cybersecurity, accept supervision from the government and public, and bear social responsibility (Article 9). Network operators shall provide technical support and assistance to state organs related to national security (Article 28).
National Intelligence Law	2017	Organizations and citizens shall support and cooperate with state intelligence work (Articles 7, 14).
National Security Law of Hong Kong	2020	Criminalizes separatism, subversion, terrorism, and collusion with foreign countries or "external elements" deemed to endanger national security. Applies to "any institution, organization or individual" in Hong Kong (Article 6), or outside of China (Article 29).
Antiforeign Sanctions Law	2021	Organizations/entities/individuals involved with "discriminatory restrictive measures against Chinese citizens and organizations" may be subject to countermeasures (Article 4). Organizations/entities/individuals must implement antiforeign sanction measures (Article 11). Organizations/entities/individuals must not aid in implementing sanctions imposed by other countries (Article 12).
Data Security Law	2021	Expects departments, industry organizations, enterprises, and individuals to protect data security (Article 9). Prohibits domestic entities from providing critical data to foreign countries (Article 31).

Sources: Xinhua News Agency Wire 2014; Standing Committee of the National People's Congress 2015; Creemers, Webster and Triolo 2018; Tanner 2017; National People's Congress 2021; DigiChina 2021.
"Data Security Law of the PRC," *Anquan neican* (Internal security documents), June 12, 2021.

Table 5. China's political economy from a comparative analytical perspective

Theory/ concept	Core attributes	Theory as compared with reform-era China
Modernization theory	Market-driven industrialization and urbanization More education Growth of middle class Democratization	*Typically applied to 1980s to early 2000s* Key differences: More state activism Absence of democratization
Developmental state	Prioritization of economic growth in late industrializers Strong state capacity and bureaucracy State guidance of market economy Industrial policy Directed credit to private industry Dominant firms privately owned Export-oriented with some import substitution	*Typically applied to 1990s onwards* Key differences: Banking system privileges SOEs over (more productive) private firms Far greater openness to and reliance on FDI More corruption/predation Much higher inequality
Post-socialist transitions	Rapid marketization of command economy Privatization of state-owned enterprises Collapse of ruling communist party Barriers to deeper reforms due to vested interests	*Typically applied to 1990s and early 2000s* Key differences: Gradual reform rather than shock therapy Continued political monopoly of Communist Party
State capitalism	Mixed economy with large private sector State ownership of strategic industries Industrial policy targeted at SOEs SOEs face soft budget constraint Outbound FDI led by SOEs and sovereign wealth funds	*General fit during 2000s*
Fascism	Reaction to failure of previous models Prioritization of national political goals, including international status Quest for economic self-sufficiency (autarky) State control over private capital Mass mobilization and militarism More totalitarian than authoritarian	*Some similarities with party-state capitalism since late 2000s* Key differences: Socialist ideology Reform rather than rejection of previous model Continued strong ties to global economy

Source: Compiled by authors.

5.4 Comparative Analytical Implications

Having delineated the evolution of China's reform-era political economy, we revisit how it compares with the conventional models of political economy discussed in Section 2. Table 5 summarizes the core attributes of each of the theories and indicates the extent to which China's developmental experience mirrors or departs from them during different periods.

During the first two decades of reform, high growth fueled by rural industrialization, urbanization, and private-sector development led observers to draw parallels with *modernization theory*. China "modernized" economically, but the process has been much more dirigiste than the Anglo-American paths to modernity. Furthermore, by the late 2000s, most political scientists had shifted away from deliberating about the prospects for democratization in China in favor of qualifying its form of authoritarianism with various adjectives (Tsai 2021). A large literature on "authoritarian resilience" pointed to the CCP's adaptive capacity (Heilmann and Perry 2011), the PRC's institutions (Truex 2016; Nathan 2003), and public legitimacy (Tang 2016). On the other hand, and particularly after the rise of Xi, scholars focused on the CCP's repressive and coercive capacity (Greitens 2016; Deng and O'Brien 2013; Ong 2022). In any case, the prospects for political liberalization, whether from the top or in response to demands from below, seem negligible.

Due to the prominent role of the state in China's political economy and its prioritization of economic growth, comparisons with the East Asian *developmental state* became more popular during the 1990s. This is not surprising given partial similarities in features such as industrial policy, export orientation, and the outcome of rapid growth. China also shares with developmental states an approach to rural modernization that features campaigns and mobilization. This observation is a more recent addition to the developmental state literature given its traditional emphasis on technocratic management, but recent research has uncovered these commonalities and evidence of policy learning in the East Asian region (Looney 2020). After the first two decades of reform, when the CCP's growth priorities shifted from export-oriented, labor-intensive manufacturing to technology-driven growth and large-scale efforts to direct investment to underdeveloped parts of the country, the National Development and Reform Commission (NDRC) took on a significant role in directing development, perhaps more similar to the developmental state's "pilot" ministries. But, as we have argued, these developmental goals are subservient to political ones in a way that distinguishes the Chinese economic model.

Overall, significant differences between China's developmental trajectory and that of its postwar regional neighbors call into question the empirical fit of the developmental state. Even though China engaged in industrial policy, its state-controlled banking system has consistently prioritized lending to

SOEs rather than the more productive private sector (Lardy 2019; Tsai 2017). Another key contrast is that reform-era China has been far more open to FDI than other developmental states (Huang 2003; Kroeber 2016). The outcomes also differ in meaningful ways. Japan and the newly industrializing countries grew rapidly during the postwar decades while maintaining relatively equitable distribution of income (Haggard 1989). By contrast, China's Gini coefficient and regional inequality indicators have ballooned at an alarming pace in the course of marketization (Jones, Li, & Owen 2003; Wang 2008). Corruption and predatory behavior on the part of state agents has also been more pervasive in China than in the developmental states (Pei 2016; Pempel 2021).

The developmental state model described the experience of rapid industrializers in East Asia during their transformations, but those political economies evolved significantly in the process. Politically, authoritarian regimes in Korea and Taiwan opened to political competition and multiparty democracy. Slater and Wong (2022) argue that ruling parties democratized "from strength" rather than weakness, as ruling parties expected they could compete and win in elections based on their strong developmental records. Economically, the Korean and Japanese economies both experienced crises. Korea was hit badly by the Asian Financial Crisis in 1997–98, which dealt a fatal blow to many national champions and exposed the extent of resource misallocation and corruption there (Kang 2002; Pempel 1999). Japan experienced an asset bubble and subsequent burst leading to what is typically called the country's "lost decades" of low or no growth, deflation, and ballooning national debt (Funabashi & Kushner 2015). The scholars cited here have analyzed these political and economic outcomes as evolutions of a developmental state model, identifying how features of developmental statism explain the model's demise or dismantlement.

China is also an outlier relative to other countries studied in the *post-socialist transitions* research agenda.[12] Instead of radical marketization, its experimental and gradualist approach to reform delayed mass privatization of SOEs until the third decade of reform – and then the largest SOEs in strategic sectors were promoted by the state. Although China has confronted political barriers to deepening reform due to vested interests like its Russian and Eastern/Central European counterparts, the continued monopoly of political power by the Chinese Communist Party is a key overarching difference. In this respect, referring to contemporary China as "post-socialist" is somewhat misleading.

---

[12] The other notable exception is Vietnam, which shares more similarities with China's reform process (Kerkvliet, Chan, & Unger 1998).

It no longer has a command economy, but remains ruled by a party that identifies with socialist principles such as "common prosperity." As Xi Jinping exhorted at the 20th Party Congress, "We must never waver in upholding the basic tenets of Marxism, the overall leadership of the Party, and socialism with Chinese characteristics" (Xi 2022). This is another example of how China's mode of political economy is not well described by familiar terms such as "socialist" and "post-socialist" (Naughton 2017).

As discussed, *state capitalism* aligns the most closely with China's political economy during the 2000s. Its mixed economy included a large private sector, alongside state ownership of strategic industries; industrial policy targeted at SOEs (including access to subsidized credit from the state banking system); and dominance of outward FDI by SOEs and sovereign wealth funds. These features persist, but since the late 2000s China's political economy has evolved into a variant of state capitalism marked by party-state activism in reaction to various political, economic, and social risks produced by the domestic and global expansion of capitalism. While steeped in normative theory, earlier debates among continental theorists over the implications of state capitalism/fascism offer comparative historical insight into the dynamics underlying the transition from one type of capitalism to another. By considering fascism as a historically specific episode rather than a regime type or a coherent system of political economy, we call attention to its rise as a reaction to political-economic crisis and its emphasis on steering capital to serve national political goals. Pollock and his peers bore witness to profound empirical changes in state-society and political-economic relations, partially in reaction to "the general crisis of capitalism" (Bukharin 1934). By the same token, the emergence of party-state capitalism in contemporary China marks a tangible shift from its preceding and more familiar form of state capitalism.

Fascist governments approached political economy in a manner similar to party-state capitalism. Principally, the imperative of political control by the state (rather than focusing on the mode of ownership) and the prioritization of national political goals over all else are common features. Beyond this similarity of a state-securitized economy, China's contemporary model of party-state capitalism differs from other core attributes of twentieth-century fascism. First, the political conditions are fundamentally different. While fascist movements were radically rightwing and anticommunist, socialist ideology remains salient in China, even as generations of party leadership have adapted its interpretation and policy objectives over time. The CCP emphasizes continuity with party-led reform rather than a radical break with the past. In terms of tactics, there has been reinvigoration of campaign-style governance that typified the Mao era

(Perry 2021). But the scope of mass mobilization is much more circumscribed than under fascism, and while daily life in China became subject to greater surveillance after the outbreak of Covid-19, it is not militarized in a fascist manner.

Finally, China's quest for economic self-sufficiency to reduce reliance on foreign goods and technology resonates in part with the appeal of autarky during the 1930s, but in practice, its economy remains deeply entwined with global supply chains. As the world's largest exporter since 2009, China is not "decoupling" from global capitalism. However, under party-state capitalism the CCP's fundamentally political mandate to promote its survival extends beyond the territorial borders of mainland China, commanding compliance with party-defined limits on politically acceptable discourse and economic behavior. Party-state capitalism has created its own effects in global capitalism, which we explore in the next section.

6 External Backlash Against China's Model

> The malleability of capitalism is its great strength. Crises of capitalism are as old as capitalism itself. Yet, each time, capitalism has survived, reforming and adapting itself to new challenges.
>
> Dani Rodrik (2021: 825)

We conclude this Element by narrating how China's new model has interacted with global capitalism. First, we note that party-state capitalism has generated backlash, especially among wealthy nations with deep economic ties to China. In a manner that resonates with the classic security dilemma in international relations, actions taken to reduce perceived threats in the economic realm have unintentionally created a downward spiral in retaliatory actions that render all involved actors less secure (Pearson, Rithmire, & Tsai 2022). In the conclusion that follows, we situate China's reevaluation of its political economy and engagement with global capitalism into broader comparative and international perspectives on the politics of development models and current trends in global capitalism. We see China's evolution as a piece of, and sometimes a driver of, a political reaction to the domestic and global problems of contemporary capitalism. While this Element is primarily about China's experience and its unique embrace of the party-state as a response to the perceived need for risk management, it shares in the general tide. Changes in China's model are part of a dynamic global story, in which we observe a reevaluation of capitalism and global market relations.

The core features of China's party-state capitalism model have reverberated internationally, causing severe and sustained backlash, particularly from the US and European countries. Critiques of China have also emanated from the developing world regarding the motives and impact of its Belt and Road Initiative (BRI), a massive transcontinental investment and infrastructural project introduced in 2013. On balance, however, the developmental benefits from China's engagement in overseas aid and investment are more often recognized in the Global South as compared with the perception of security risks in OECD countries.

The type and depth of conflict between China and OECD countries has taken a new turn in recent years. During most of the reform era, geostrategic issues – such as territorial disputes with Japan and in the South China Sea, Taiwan's status, and US interests in East Asia – punctuated a generally solid relationship between China and the US. Disputes over human rights have been an ongoing source of tension between China and Western countries, and featured prominently in conservative US opposition to China's accession to the WTO in the 1990s. Nonetheless, until more recently economic interdependence was more often viewed pragmatically by both the US and China as a source of common interest, and to some degree served as a balm for disputes. Constraints on conflict offered by commercial links was consistent with the influential international relations literature on liberal institutionalism, whereby economic interdependence is expected to pacify or produce cooperation (Davis & Meunier 2010; Ikenberry 2008).

As the contours of China's party-state capitalism have become more pronounced, however, its signature elements have become flashpoints in relations between China and OECD countries, and brought economic ties squarely into the realm of national security. Industrial policies, while not new in China, have become more expansive – especially Made in China 2025. Increased attention overseas has been drawn to heightened pressures on foreign companies to hew to the CCP's political line on sensitive issues such as human rights violations in Xinjiang and the status of Hong Kong and Taiwan. The passage of laws and regulations in Beijing (Table 3) also gained increasing attention outside of China, and reinforced the view that China's government is securitizing economic interactions previously embedded in and largely governed by markets. Consternation over the blurring of lines between the state and firms, evident in various forms of "financialization" as well as in new laws, has produced confusion about whether economic transactions were merely economic transactions or part of a broader security strategy driven by the CCP and in the service of its own survival.

Alarm over these trends and events existed side by side with and were perhaps amplified by other more traditional economic conflicts. Notable among these are expanded use of tools of economic statecraft (Baldwin 1985; Norris 2016), including the US-China trade war initiated by the US in 2018, and the use by the US – and more recently, China – of economic sanctions intended to respond to myriad complaints about issues such as market access, antidumping, and so on (Hufbauer & Jung 2020). These more traditional tools of trade conflict or economic competition were not directly tied to concerns over China's party-dominated economic model. In the late 2010s, however, unlike these more traditional conflicts, alarm about China's model has converted many elements of economic interdependence into national security concerns. Scholars have noted trends toward "weaponization" of an economically interconnected world, which is evident in conflict between China and OECD countries (e.g., Brooks 2017; Farrell & Newman 2021). Our discussion highlights the role played by domestic sources – changes in China's economic development model – in producing conflict in novel terrains.

Backlash against China from the US and Europe has taken myriad forms, and accumulated much analysis (e.g., Goldstein 2020, Hanemann & Huotari 2018). We describe four of the most prominent here: 1) restricting FDI from China; 2) banning Chinese technology and surveillance firms; 3) new initiatives to counter the "China threat"; and 4) designing industrial policy to reduce reliance on Chinese technology.

6.1 Restricting Chinese FDI

Western countries have reconsidered the benefits of FDI flows from China, particularly in sectors considered sensitive and of potential dual use. FDI from China in the US began to take off in 2009, and skyrocketed upward from about $15 billion in 2015 to $16 billion in 2016, before plummeting to negligible levels by 2018 (Rhodium China Investment Monitor n.d.). (Levels of FDI from US firms in China remained relatively steady, at around $12 billion during that period.) A similar spike occurred in the EU and UK during those years (Rhodium China Investment Monitor n.d.). Although a pullback of FDI from China reflected in part calculations by Chinese firms about a broad range of risks, one such risk was clearly the increased government monitoring of such deals, whether mergers and acquisitions or greenfield investment.

In the US, the Committee on Foreign Investment in the US (CFIUS) was set up in 1975, and then strengthened to scrutinize investment from Japan – a military ally – in 1988 (Graham & Marchick 2006). By 2015, concerns over Chinese industrial policies designed to guarantee supplies of critical goods were heightened enough for the Obama administration to invoke CFIUS tools to restrict acquisition of the US subsidiary of German chip machine supplier Aixtron by a Chinese firm (Henning 2016). In summer 2018, a bipartisan bill (the Foreign Investment Risk Review Modernization Act, FIRRMA) expanded CFIUS rules that previously required a review only when a foreign investor sought a *controlling* stake, to instead require a review of *any stake* sought in companies "with substantial business in the US" if they are involved in "emerging technologies" or "critical infrastructure" (US Department of Treasury 2018).

European and East Asian governments similarly raised alarms over Chinese acquisitions of critical infrastructure at this time (Mozur & Ewing 2016). In the sensitive semiconductor sector, Taiwan and South Korea initiated steps to prohibit or restrict Chinese acquisitions and prevent transfer of intellectual property and engineering talent to China (President's Council 2017). Many OECD countries, starting as early as the late 2010s, passed legislation to establish or buttress investment reviews. Prior to 2020, France, Germany, and Italy raised the possibility of an EU-wide screening process, while the Australian Foreign Investment Review Board (FIRB) announced its intent to increase scrutiny of Chinese private companies looking to buy Australian assets (European Commission 2017; Grigg 2019). Tellingly, in justifying a strengthened review process for proposed investments from China, advocates frequently invoked the perceived indistinctness between Chinese firms, including private firms, and the CCP. As a representative of the Australian FIRB bluntly stated, there "is no such thing as a private company in China" (Grigg 2019).

6.2 Targeting Chinese Firms

Concurrent with strengthening the institutional processes for review of Chinese investments, the US government went further to target specific firms for their presumed threat to national security. In a high-profile case, the US government targeted telecommunications giant Huawei – a firm with opaque ownership structures that while technically "private," was widely viewed as closely tied to the Chinese military and the CCP. A 2012 report in the US Congress accused Huawei (and fellow telecommunications giant ZTE) of "economic and foreign espionage by a foreign nation-state already known to be a major perpetrator of cyber espionage" (US House Intelligence Committee 2012). Seven years later, the 2018 National Defense Authorization Act prohibited federal agencies from procuring products/services from Huawei or ZTE. Placement of Huawei on the US Department of Commerce's "unreliable entity" list in 2019 deprived Huawei of semiconductor chips as punishment. US government nervousness over large Chinese firms has escalated, especially in technology sectors, as they expanded access to the US. Even ByteDance, the privately owned parent of social media platform TikTok, was targeted by the Trump and Biden administrations as a national security threat due to suspected ties with the Chinese government.

Similarly, while human rights violations have long been a source of tensions between China and Western countries, backlash in this arena also has been directed at Chinese firms. Governmental bans on use of surveillance equipment from Hikvision and Dahua, for example, have been framed in the context of their use in Xinjiang. Because their products are also being used by autocracies along the Digital Silk Road, human rights observers regard their exports as "exporting digital authoritarianism" on the part of the Chinese government (Polyakova & Merole 2019). As such, security concerns are also infused with ethical critiques.

6.3 New Initiatives to Counter the "China Threat"

In response to perceptions of a "China threat," a third cluster of actions entails novel institutions and rules for the state to protect private sector assets of OECD countries. The US government has been the most proactive in this regard, with legislative proposals to screen more closely outbound US investment to China. The proposal that has advanced farthest is a potential National Critical Capabilities Defense Act, which would establish an interagency group under the Office of the US Trade Representative to screen transactions by US businesses in "countries of concern" and where "national critical capabilities" are at stake. Advocates argue that without such a control tool, investments can lead to the transfer of sensitive (or potentially sensitive) technologies, outsourcing of critical production, and obscured supply chains (Hanemann et al. 2022). While criticism of US investment into China is not new, in the past objections largely focused on the accompanying outsourcing of US jobs, or the export of technology itself, rather than on the need to screen outward foreign direct investment for national security reasons. We view such action as an unprecedented effort by the contemporary American state to constrain capital movements, transgressing the bounds of what was previously deemed acceptable statist control of private property.

Also in the US, the Department of Justice in 2018 introduced the "China Initiative," another extreme measure aimed in part to respond to China's model and the blurring of state and the economy, as well as society. The China Initiative was premised on the idea that economic espionage and theft of intellectual property, especially related to dual-use technologies, as well as CCP influence in universities, pose a national security threat to the US (Lewis 2021). As FBI Director Christopher Wray put it, "China from a counterintelligence perspective represents the broadest, most challenging threat we face at this time ... because with them it's a whole of state effort" (quoted in Lutz 2018).[13] Echoing this

---

[13] Wray's "whole-of-society" approach to confronting China echoes Xi Jinping's (2018b) view that the party should lead a "whole-of-society approach" to creating a cyber superpower.

position, the US Attorney for the District of Massachusetts Andrew Lelling contended, "If you are collaborating with any Chinese entity, whether it's a university or a business, you are giving that technology to the Chinese government" (cited in Lewis 2021: 178). Prior to its end in 2022, the Initiative directed largely unfettered scrutiny at Chinese nationals and Chinese-Americans, resulting in investigative overreach and racial profiling.

A new transatlantic institution also has been established: the US-EU Trade and Technology Council. The Council's aim is to coordinate among allies for standards on artificial intelligence, quantum computing, and biotechnology products. These areas are subjects of China's industrial policies that, among other things, bundle state funds and private capital in an opaque manner – suggesting to Western governments similar sorts of threats from party-state capitalism driving the suite of policies discussed here. Such initiatives evoke the notion that OECD countries are responding to calls for a Western alliance that is "[l]ike NATO, but for economic threats" (Vinci 2020).

6.4 Industrial Policy to Reduce Reliance on Chinese Technology

A fourth tranche of initiatives focuses on strengthening OECD countries' own industries to better compete with the perceived threat from China, and Chinese industrial policies, at home and overseas. Industrial policy, and more broadly national innovation systems, are not unknown in the West, especially in Europe (Asheim & Gertler 2005; Nelson 1993). Indeed, Made in China 2025 was fashioned in part after Germany's "Industry 4.0" plan. The US government, with an eye to competition with China, engaged legislation that nodded to industrial policy to an unusual degree in the form of the US Innovation and Competition Act of 2021. The nearly 2,400-page, $250 billion bill is designed to foster US semiconductor production, scientific research, the development of artificial intelligence, and space exploration in the face of growing economic, technological, and military competition from China (US Congress 2021). It calls for "catalytic" investments in these sectors, and extensive government procurement efforts to create markets for these goods. Even Republicans, who might be expected to eschew "statist" economic moves, favored the bill.

Significant legislative spending bills, such as the CHIPS (creating helpful incentives to produce semiconductors) and Science Act of 2022, were designed to address fears that China's overseas investments in the developing world through the BRI would be leveraged for Chinese influence. The Biden administration in 2021 proposed the Build Back Better World (B3W), adopted by the G7 to build infrastructure in developing countries. Later that year, the EU launched its own Global Gateway Initiative with largely the same purpose:

competing with the BRI (European Commission 2021). In the last year of the Trump administration, the US State Department launched a "Clean Network" initiative to persuade US allies and telecommunications firms worldwide to exclude Chinese 5G providers from their networks. The effort was intended to preclude Chinese vendors for security reasons, and also to enable US entrants in the sector (Rithmire & Han 2021).

Taken together, these measures to counter the perceived China threat have deepened China's preexisting sense of insecurity. While the security dilemma in international relations theory focuses on military competition, the emergence of party-state capitalism in response to perceived internal and external threats (Table 5) has elicited similar dynamics in the economic realm. As detailed elsewhere, the measures that China has taken to enhance its own sense of security have had the perverse effect of triggering counterreactions, especially from OECD countries, which fuel a downward spiral of increasingly hostile economic policy measures (Pearson, Rithmire, & Tsai 2022).

7 Conclusion: China's Development Model and Crises of Global Capitalism

By focusing on the case of China, this Element probes the ways in which models of capitalism evolve, emphasizing the primacy of politics in organizing the political economy (Berman 2019), and the potential for evolution of development models. In many respects the case of post-Mao China is unusual in the contemporary era, with the party-state's determination to be at the helm of steering economic development. Still, China's state is by no means alone in responding to ills resulting from its model of capitalism. In the West, scholars have characterized many democratic countries as nearing a tipping point due to dislocation and inequality. These trends are seen as endangering the social compact between capital and labor that originated in the industrial revolution (Boix 2019; Przeworski 2019). The related literature is rich in its assessment of economic tensions – notably wage stagnation, economic inequality – and the political and class cleavages evident in industrial democracies (Hall 2020; Kahler & Lake 2013). Often tensions are seen to have been deepened by, and led to popular backlash against, globalization (Streeck 2014).

China's reformers have similarly grappled with these issues. The "New Left" critics of marketization in the 1990s were deeply concerned about the erosion of socialist values, the rise of inequality, and potential instability. For much of the post-Mao era, economic growth – achieved largely through engagement with the global economy – remained the paramount objective. The party-state assumed a confident posture that it could manage resulting challenges, such as inequality. However, mounting unease with the downsides of capitalism in part drove Xi Jinping's proposal for "common prosperity" in the summer of 2021. While Mao Zedong and Deng Xiaoping used the term earlier in reference to economic wellbeing, under Xi "common prosperity" has become a broader initiative to ameliorate the social, cultural, and environmental damage stemming from decades of unprecedented (and unbalanced) growth. In addition to a rural revitalization campaign to eliminate poverty and relocation of manufacturing to inland provinces, common prosperity encompasses disciplinary policies that reflect Xi's particular vision of "social morals and traditional virtues" for Chinese society. These campaign-style restrictions range from the banning of private tutoring companies and limits on online gaming to the censuring of celebrity influencers for "improper" content (Koty 2022). Also under the banner of common prosperity is a pledge to achieve carbon neutrality by 2060. "Common prosperity" has arguably become a catch-all initiative to fix problems perceived to be associated with rapid growth and lax regulation of markets.

Overall, China's government has been drawn to react to problems similar to those found in Western capitalist economies and, in the case of environmental degradation, found worldwide. Even before the global financial crisis, then Premier Wen Jiabao declared to the 5th Session of the 10th National People's Congress that "China's economy has huge problems, which are still unstable, unbalanced, uncoordinated and unsustainable structural problems" (PRC Central Government Portal 2007). While many of the catalysts that triggered adjustments in China's model in the mid-2000s originated in concerns shared by many capitalist economies, a heightened perception of domestic and external threat prompted the shift to party-state capitalism as a solution.

Markets are double edged from Beijing's perspective. On the one hand, they support the state's goals of enhancing productivity, innovation, and exports. On the other hand, party-state capitalism reflects suspicion that markets and capital (especially private capital) creates security vulnerabilities that will undermine the state. As Xi noted in a speech to the CCP Politburo in April 2022,

> In a socialist market economy, capital is an important link in driving the concentration and allocation of factors of production, and an important force in promoting social productivity, [therefore] we have to take advantage of the positive effects of capital. Meanwhile, we must recognize that capital has a profit-seeking nature. Capital will bring inestimable damage to our social and economic development in the absence of regulation and restriction (CCP News 2022).

While China's party-state capitalism seeks to curb the undesirable effects of markets, the new model has inspired a vigorous backlash by advanced capitalist countries. Even more far-reaching than the specific steps taken in OECD countries to counter the perceived threat from China, the rise of party-state capitalism has prompted Western governments to reassess their commitments to certain foundations of globalization and interdependence. Akin to the oil shocks of the 1970s, a "political China shock" has bled into the national security architecture of wealthy Western governments and produced de facto challenges to economic interdependence. These are layered on top of other trends endemic to Western capitalist systems, including domestic political polarization, trends away from multilateralism, and an "economic China shock" blamed for hollowing out much of the US' manufacturing base (Autor, Dorn, & Hanson 2016). A major external cause is the perception of threat from China's economic model. Yet the following two trends specifically mirror China's party-state capitalism. First is the growing preference, seen in policy proposals, for the state in capitalist systems to steer private capital toward national security goals. This response is visible in restrictions on incoming and outgoing capital, as well as the greater appeal (quite new outside of wartime in the US) of enacting industrial policies to compete on national security grounds.

Second is the increasing calls for the "decoupling" of Western economies, in both supplies of goods and capital, from China. Interdependence with China through market coordination has come to be viewed as risky on multiple fronts. To be sure, the domestic economic risks of interdependence with China have been voiced for some time – especially loss of jobs due to outsourcing of manufacturing and loss of competitiveness due to theft of intellectual property (Autor, Dorn & Hanson 2016). But arguments in favor of producing at home, or in trusted networks, became more fervent during national security debates over interaction with Chinese firms in areas now considered "securitized" (Beeny 2018). Particularly sensitive is the idea that US firms could be aiding the development of China's military, intelligence, and surveillance capabilities (Bade 2022). Moreover, during the Covid-19 pandemic, deep dependence on Chinese-origin supply chains came under intense scrutiny and was seen as a threat to health security. In a similar fashion, China's formulation of a "dual circulation" strategy indicates a reciprocal mistrust of international markets. The strategy's origins predate the urgent debates in the West about decoupling,[14] but the party-state capitalism model

---

[14] Note that one half of "dual" circulation is the "great international circulation" – visions of continued, if decreasing, reliance on international markets for exports as well as for technology acquisition. The emphasis on increasing "domestic circulation" originated with the Global

has reinforced calls for internalizing the sources of industrial upgrading (Lin & Wang 2021). Although debates about the concrete meaning and policies for decoupling are occurring in both China and OECD countries, the prominence of the discussion crystallizes the degree to which China's party-state capitalism has generated reconsideration of the value of global interdependence, perhaps portending the "death knell" of globalization (Slobodian 2020).

This raises the question, in turn, of whether Beijing's reactions to the problems attributed to capitalism presage a reversal of market reforms domestically (Minzner 2018). Will China's private sector be progressively emasculated and nationalized, as occurred during the 1950s? Critics of Xi's anticorruption campaign and crackdowns on private entrepreneurs recall the persecution of "bourgeois capitalists" during the "Five-Antis" campaign (1952) that charged China's largest capitalists with the five evils of bribery, tax evasion, theft of state property, cheating on government contracts, and stealing economic information. Contemporary media reports and rumors of Chinese CEOs in political trouble have indeed had a chilling effect on critical statements and ostentatious behaviors. However, we do not believe that the intention is to revert to Mao-era socialism, as the party-state recognizes its dependence on private-sector dynamism to help China achieve its goals of technological innovation and self-reliance. This is readily evident in the surveillance industry. China's surveillance infrastructure initially depended on foreign technology imports in the 1990s, but it has since been overtaken by domestic privately owned surveillance giants that dominate global rankings of security firms (Huang & Tsai 2022). In the digital age, even dirigiste autocracies are compelled to allow foreign and/or private firms to supply frontier technology because it is well established that the public sector lacks innovative capacity. After all, the logic of extending state capital to the nonstate sector through government guidance funds in Made in China 2025 was precisely that SOEs would not be on the forefront of innovation (Chen & Rithmire 2020).

Instead of diagnosing party-state capitalism as a swing back to the "state" away from the "market" (Lardy 2019), we have emphasized the political imperative. Party-state capitalism is neither a return to state socialism nor an elimination of markets, but rather the embrace of public and private ownership and the use of market mechanisms to bolster political control. While such a

___

Financial Crisis of 2008–09, as China's government became more aware of risks of dependence on export markets, and became even more deeply enshrined as part of Made in China 2025 (Garcia-Herrero 2021). Moreover, food and energy security have been concerns to some degree throughout the reform era.

formulation sounds oxymoronic in classic Western theories of capitalism, in Xi Jinping's formulation there is no inconsistency, at least in terms of ideological presentation. He reasoned as follows in the CCP's primary theoretical journal, *Seeking Truth* (*Qiushi* 求是):

> The socialist market economy is a great creation of our party. Because it is a socialist market economy, it will inevitably produce several kinds of capital. While there are several differences between capital in a capitalist society and capital in a socialist society, capital is always about chasing profits . . . We must explore how, within a context of socialist market economy, to maximize the positive role of capital while effectively controlling its negative role . . . This means regulating the behavior of capital [and] not allowing 'capital predators' to act recklessly, but also facilitating capital as a factor of production. (Xi 2022)

Lastly, though we have emphasized a resurgent state and political imperative, we caution against assuming that the power of capital has been rendered wholly subservient to the state. The reality is that Chinese firms, both large and small, continue to pursue profits amidst an emboldened role for the party-state as economic steward (Heberer & Schubert 2020). At times this pursuit of profits and innovation forces the state to tolerate private sector autonomy, as in the case of the surveillance sector already discussed. Other times, nonstate and even state actors pursue their own objectives in ways that subvert the party-state's interests. Even as the Xi administration has emphasized the need for taming capital, firms and individuals cloak their own pursuits in the language of the state's goals while behaving in ways that are economically or politically costly for the regime. Much of the capital that flowed out of China after the global financial crisis was capital flight, as evident in the CCP's focus on repatriating assets and the "criminals" who captured them (Rithmire 2022). Clearly, when the state is intolerant of instability, moral hazard is present as firms recognize opportunities to benefit from the state's largesse with expectations of bailouts or impunity (Chen & Rithmire 2020; Rithmire & Chen 2021).

Capital is not docile in the face of state intervention. Just as the CCP seeks to harness private capital to achieve its goals, capital makes use of state policy to realize its own. Rather than declaring one side victor over the other, students of China's political economy ought to take both the party-state and capitalism as integral elements of the model and investigate how incentives and behaviors have changed as politics has become the priority.

We conclude this Element with suggestions for an ongoing research agenda focused on three areas relevant to China's political economy model.[15] First, although we have largely provided evidence for the strengthened role of the party-state in China's economy, we and others recognize that this role has sometimes modulated. We expect ongoing ebbs and flows in party-state influence on firms and sectors. Yet we have little systematic understanding of what leads to that fluctuation between liberalization and control (*fang* 放 and *shou* 收). Historically, scholars of post-1949 China have depicted the dynamic as a continuous undulation in the relationship between state and society (Pye 1992) and cycles of liberalization and retrenchment (Baum 1994), sometimes driven by elite preferences and sometimes as a reaction to societal conditions. Such driving forces will remain pertinent as both leadership changes and economic crisis, as well as pushback from business and international circles, come to the fore. Understanding the main drivers of such flux will remain of great interest.

Because a main driver of this oscillation in the political climate often emerges in response to conditions "on the ground," a second research agenda should probe the actual impact of China's new "model," and seek to address a number of unresolved questions: How does party-state capitalism impact crucial economic variables, including those important to the party-state itself – notably innovation, growth, and employment? How does it impact, if at all, China's expressed commitments to environmental sustainability and the country's role in addressing ecological crises emanating from capitalism worldwide? In what ways do the trends toward securitization and financialization described here affect firms positively, negatively, or in a mixed fashion? To what extent does the insertion of party personnel into firms have a discernible impact on business decisions or corporate governance?

Finally, what is the international impact of China's party-state capitalism beyond OECD countries? This Element has pointed to the perceived security implications of China's outward economic trade, aid, and investment, and US and European efforts to counterbalance these. Yet a broader agenda should seek to understand how, and how much, the drivers of party-state capitalism are infused into China's expanded role in the Global South. Existing studies have focused on ways in which China's overseas activities signify efforts to expand its soft power (Morgan 2019; Repnikova 2022). Yet are these successes (and failures) related directly to party-state capitalism, suggesting a deeper intention at overseas influence through a "China Model"? To the degree that an apparent China model

---

[15] Considerable research already exists in some of these areas, although not always tied in origin or implications to China's development model. Our references to other literature here are merely suggestive rather than exhaustive.

is salient to communities in the Global South, is it regarded as attractive or negative – or again, as trivial (Fuchs & Rudyak 2019; Patey 2020; Ratigan 2021; Wang, Pearson, & McCauley 2022)? How do these perceptions join with discussions of whether China is exporting authoritarianism more broadly? Just as we have observed the evolution of China's political economy in reaction to domestic and global forces, so, too, will party-state capitalism generate its own effects and forces of change. Those dynamics are neither predetermined nor contained within China's borders, and therefore merit productive attention from a wide range of social scientists.

List of Abbreviations

B3W	Build Back Better World
BRI	Belt and Road Initiative
CCP	Chinese Communist Party
CFIUS	Committee on Foreign Investment in the United States
EU	European Union
FDI	Foreign direct investment
FIRB	Foreign Investment Review Board (in Australia)
FIRRMA	Foreign Investment Risk Review Modernization Act
G7	Group of Seven countries
GATT	General Agreement on Tariffs and Trade
IMF	International Monetary Fund
IPO	Initial public offering
MLP	Medium- and Long-term Plan
MNC	Multinational corporation
NATO	North Atlantic Treaty Organization
NDRC	National Development and Reform Commission
NBA	National Basketball Association
OECD	Organisation for Economic Co-operation and Development
PRC	People's Republic of China
RMB	Renminbi (currency of China)
SASAC	State-owned Assets Supervision and Administration Commission
SOE	State-owned enterprise
SPD	Socialist Democratic Party (of Germany)
TVE	Township and village enterprise
USSR	Union of Soviet Socialist Republics
WTO	World Trade Organization

References

Almanac of China's Finance and Banking. 2017. *Zhongguo jinrong nianjian* [Almanac of China's Finance and Banking]. Beijing: China Finance Press.

Almond, Gabriel and Sidney Verba. 1963. *The Civic Culture: Political Attitudes and Democracy in Five Nations*. Princeton: Princeton University Press.

Amsden, Alice H. 1992. *Asia's Next Giant: South Korea and Late Industrialization*. Oxford: Oxford University Press.

Amsden, Alice H. 2001. *The Rise of "the Rest": Challenges to the West from Late-Industrializing Economies*. New York: Oxford University Press.

Ang, Yuen Yuen. 2016. *How China Escaped the Poverty Trap*. Ithaca, NY: Cornell University Press.

Ang, Yuen Yuen. 2020. *China's Gilded Age: The Paradox of Economic Boom and Vast Corruption*. New York: Cambridge University Press.

Asheim, Bjorn T., and Meric S. Gertler. 2005. "The Geography of Innovation," in J. Fagerberg, D. Mowery and R. Nelson (eds.), *The Oxford Handbook of Innovation*. Oxford: Oxford University Press, 291–317.

Åslund, Anders. 1995. *How Russia Became a Market Economy*. Washington, DC: Brookings Institution Press.

Autor, David, David Dorn, and Gordon Hanson. 2016. "The China Shock: Learning from Labor Market Adjustment to Large Changes in Trade." *Annual Review of Economics* 8(10): 205–40.

Bade, Gavin. 2022. "White House Split Delays Plans for Investment Controls on China." *Politico*. March 7. www.politico.com/news/2022/03/07/white-house-investment-rules-china-00014496.

Bai, Chong-Eng, Chang-Tai Hsieh, and Michael Song Zheng. 2019. "Special Deals with Chinese Characteristics." NBER Working Papers 25839. National Bureau of Research, Inc. May. www.nber.org/papers/w25839.

Baldwin, David A. 1985. *Economic Statecraft*. Princeton: Princeton University Press.

Baum, Richard. 1994. *Burying Mao: Chinese Politics in the Age of Deng Xiaoping*. Princeton: Princeton University Press.

Beeny, Tara. 2018. "Supply Chain Vulnerabilities from China in U.S. Federal Information and Communications Technology." Report prepared for the U.S.-China Economic and Security Review Commission. Alexandria, VA: Interos Solutions.

Béja, Jean-Philippe. 2019. "Xi Jinping's China: Marching Toward a Chinese Fascism?" *Pouvoirs* 169(2): 117–28.

Belesky, Paul, and Geoffrey Lawrence. 2019. "Chinese State Capitalism and Neomercantilism in the Contemporary Food Regime: Contradictions, Continuity, and Change." *Journal of Peasant Studies* 49(6): 1119–41.

Berend, Ivan T. 2006. *An Economic History of Twentieth-Century Europe.* Cambridge: Cambridge University Press.

Berezin, Mabel. 2019. "Fascism and Populism: Are They Useful Categories for Comparative Sociological Analysis?" *Annual Review of Sociology* 45(1): 345–61.

Berman, Sheri. 2009. "The Primacy of Economics versus the Primacy of Politics: Understanding the Ideological Dynamics of the Twentieth Century." *Perspectives on Politics* 7(3): 561–78.

Berman, Sheri. 2019. *Democracy and Dictatorship in Europe.* Oxford: Oxford University Press.

Bhagwati, Jagdish. 2004. *In Defense of Globalization.* Oxford: Oxford University Press.

Blanchette, Jude. 2019. "Against Atrophy: Party Organisations in Private Firms." *Made in China Journal.* April 18. https://madeinchinajournal.com/2019/04/18/against-atrophy-party-organisations-in-private-firms/.

Bloom, Peter. 2016. *Authoritarian Capitalism in the Age of Globalization.* Cheltenham: Edward Elgar.

Boix, Carles. 2019. *Democratic Capitalism at the Crossroads: Technological Change and the Future of Politics.* Princeton: Princeton University Press.

Brandt, Loren, and Thomas G. Rawski. 2022. "China's Great Boom as a Historical Process," in Debin Ma and Richard Von Glahn (eds.), *The Cambridge Economic History of China.* Cambridge: Cambridge University Press, pp. 775–828. https://doi.org/10.1017/9781108348485.022.

Brandt, Loren, and Eric Thun. 2010. "The Fight for the Middle: Upgrading, Competition, and Industrial Development in China." *World Development* 38(11): 1555–74.

Bremmer, Ian. 2010. *The End of the Free Market: Who Wins the War Between States and Corporations?* New York: Penguin Portfolio.

Breznitz, Dan, and Michael Murphree. 2011. *Run of the Red Queen: Government, Innovation, Globalization, and Economic Growth in China.* New Haven, CT: Yale University Press.

Brooks, Rosa. 2017. *How Everything Became War and the Military Became Everything: Tales from the Pentagon.* New York: Simon & Schuster.

Buchanan, James, Robert Tollison, and Gordon Tullock. 1980. *Toward a Theory of the Rent-Seeking Society.* College Station: Texas A&M Press.

Bukharin, Nikolai. 1934. "Crisis of Capitalist Culture." *New Masses.* December 4. www.marxists.org/archive/bukharin/works/1934/capitalist-culture.htm.

Cai, Yongshun. 2014. *State and Agents in China*. Stanford: Stanford University Press.

Carney, Richard W. 2018. *Authoritarian Capitalism: Sovereign Wealth Funds and State-Owned Enterprises in East Asia and Beyond*. New York: Cambridge University Press.

CCP News. 2022. "Yifa guifan he yingdao woguo ziben jiankang fazhan, fahui ziben zuowei zhongyao shengchan yaosu de jiji zuoyong" [Regulate and guide the healthy development of our country's capital in accordance with the law, and give full play to the positive role of capital as an important factor of production]. May 5. http://dangjian.people.com.cn/n1/2022/0505/c117092-32414147.html.

Chandler, Alfred. 1977. *The Visible Hand: The American Revolution in American Business*. Cambridge, MA: Belknap Press.

Chen, Hao, and Meg Rithmire. 2020. "The Rise of the Investor State: State Capital in the Chinese Economy." *Studies in Comparative International Development* 55(3) (September): 257–77.

Chen, Li, Huanhuan Zheng, and Yunbo Liu. 2020. "The Hybrid Regulatory Regime in Turbulent Times: The Role of the State in China's Stock Market Crisis in 2015–2016." *Regulation and Governance*. https://doi.org/10/1111/rego.12340.

Chen, Ling. 2018. *Manipulating Globalization: The Influence of Bureaucrats on Business in China*. Stanford: Stanford University Press.

Chen, Ling. 2022. "Getting China's Political Economy Right: State, Business, and Authoritarian Capitalism." *Perspectives on Politics* 20, 4 (December): 1397–1402.

Chen, Tara Francis. 2018. "US Airlines Just Gave into China's 'Orwellian' Demands over Taiwan – Here's Every Company That's Done the Same." *Business Insider.* July 25. https://www.businessinsider.com/which-companies-have-changed-taiwan-description-china-2018-7.

China Minsheng Investment Group (CMIG). "Corporate Profile." www.cm-inv.com/en/introduce/index.htm.

China Securities Regulatory Commission (CSRC). 2018. Announcement No. 29 [2018] of the China Securities Regulatory Commission – Code of Corporate Governance of Listed Companies (2018 Revision) [上市公司治理准则(2018修订)]. (September 30). Accessed and translated April 30, 2022 at www.lawinfochina.com/display.aspx?id=29351&lib=law&SearchKeyword=&SearchCKeyword=.

Chinese Communist Party. 1999. "Decision of the Central Committee of the Communist Party of China on Major Issues Concerning the Reform and Development of State-Owned Enterprises" [in Chinese]. September 22. www.lawinfochina.com/display.aspx?lib=law&id=991&CGid.

Chinese Communist Party. 2014. "Decision of the Central Committee of the Communist Party of China on Some Major Issues Concerning Comprehensively Deepening the Reform" [full English translation]. January 16. www.china.org.cn/china/third_plenary_session/2014-01/16/content_31212602.htm. Chinese version of the Decision can be accessed at http://news.xinhuanet.com/politics/2013-11/15/c_118164235.htm.

Chinese Communist Party (CCP). 2018. "Communist Party Communiqué 2017" [in Chinese]. June 30. http://news.12371.cn/2018/06/30/ARTI153034 0432898663.shtml.

Cho, SungChan, and Philip Pilsoo Choi. 2014. "Introducing Property Tax in China as an Alternative Financing Source." *Land Use Policy* 38 (May): 580–86.

Collier, Andrew. 2022. *China's Technology War: Why Beijing Took Down its Tech Giants*. Singapore: Palgrave Macmillan.

Creemers, Rogier, Graham Webster, and Paul Triolo (trans.). 2018. "Translation: Cybersecurity Law of the People's Republic of China (Effective June 1, 2017)." https://digichina.stanford.edu/work/translation-cybersecurity-law-of-the-peoples-republic-of-china-effective-june-1-2017/

Crouch, Colin. 2005. *Capitalist Diversity and Change: Recombinant Governance and Institutional Entrepreneurs*. New York: Oxford University Press.

Culpepper, Pepper. 2015. "Structural Power and Political Science in the Post-Crisis Era." *Business and Politics* 17(3) (October): 391–409.

Davidson, Michael and Margaret M. Pearson. 2022. "Static Electricity: Institutional and Ideational Barriers to China's Electricity Market Reforms." *Studies in Comparative International Development*. https://doi.org/10.1007/s12116-022-09358-9.

Dawkins, David. 2019. "UBS Economist Forced to Apologize After 'Chinese Pig' Comments Trigger Outrage." *Forbes*. June 13. https://www.forbes.com/sites/daviddawkins/2019/06/13/ubs-economist-forced-to-apologize-after-chinese-pig-comments-trigger-outrage/.

Deng, Yanhua and Kevin J. O'Brien. 2013. "Relational Repression in China: Using Social Ties to Demobilise Protestors." *China Quarterly* 215 (September): 533–52.

Deutsch, Karl. 1966. Social Mobilization and Political Development. *American Political Science Review* 55(3) (September): 493–514.

Dickson, Bruce J. 2008. *Wealth into Power: The Communist Party's Embrace of the Private Sector*. New York: Cambridge University Press.

DigiChina. 2021. "Translation: Data Security Law of the People's Republic of China (Effective Sept. 1, 2021)." https://digichina.stanford.edu/work/translation-data-security-law-of-the-peoples-republic-of-china/.

Dikotter, Frank. 2010. *Mao's Great Famine: The History of China's Most Devastating Catastrophe, 1958–1962*. New York: Walker & Co.

Ding, X. L. 2000. "The Illicit Asset Stripping of Chinese State Firms." *The China Journal* 43 (January): 1–28.

Doner, Richard F., Bryan K. Ritchie, and Dan Slater. 2005. "Systemic Vulnerability and the Origins of Developmental States: Northeast and Southeast Asia in Comparative Perspective." *International Organization* 59(2): 327–61.

Dos Santos, Theontonio. 1970. "The Structure of Dependence." *American Economic Review* 60(2) (1970): 231–36.

Eaton, Sarah. 2016. *The Advance of the State in Contemporary China: State-Market Relations in the Reform Era*. New York: Cambridge University Press.

Economic Daily. 2018. "A Total of 1,171 Government Guidance Funds were Established in China, with a Total Target Size of 5.85 Trillion Yuan" [in Chinese]. August 21. www.xinhuanet.com/2018-08/21/c_1123299570.htm.

Economy, Elizabeth. 2018. *China's Third Revolution: Xi Jinping and the New Chinese State*. New York: Oxford University Press.

Edin, Maria. 2003. "State Capacity and Local Agent Control in China: CCP Cadre Management from a Township Perspective." *China Quarterly* 173 (March): 35–52.

Esarey, Ashley. 2021. "Propaganda as a Lens for Assessing Xi Jinping's Leadership." *Journal of Contemporary China*, Special Issue on The Xi Jinping Effect in China and Beyond (II), 30(132): 888–901.

European Commission. 2017. "Regulation of the European Parliament and of the Council Establishing a Framework for Screening of Foreign Direct Investments into the European Union." September 13. https://eur-lex.eur opa.eu/legal-content/EN/TXT/?uri=CELEX%3A52017PC0487.

European Commission. 2021. "Global Gateway: Up to €300 billion for the European Union's Strategy to Boost Sustainable Links Around the World." https://ec.europa.eu/commission/presscorner/detail/en/ip_21_6433.

Evans, Peter B. 1979. *Dependent Development: The Alliance of Multinational, State and Local Capital in Brazil*. Princeton: Princeton University Press.

Evans, Peter B. 1995. *Embedded Autonomy: States and Industrial Transformation*. Princeton: Princeton University Press.

Fang, Qin, and Yimin Wang. 2017. "Zhengce yanbian yu yuqi lujing: chuban chuanmeiye teshu guanli gu zhidu tantao" ["Policy evolvement and expected path: discussion on China's 'special management shares' in publishing industry"]. *Science-Technology & Publication* (8): 14–18.

Farrell, Henry, and Abe Newman, eds. 2021. *The Uses and Abuses of Weaponized Interdependence*. Washington, DC: Brookings Institution Press.

Feldmann, Magnus. 2019. "Global Varieties of Capitalism." *World Politics* 71(1): 162–96.

Fewsmith, Joseph. 2018. "The 19th Party Congress: Ringing in Xi Jinping's New Age." *China Leadership Monitor* 55. www.hoover.org/research/19th-party-congress-ringing-xi-jinpings-new-age.

Freed, Jamie. 2019. "As Protests Wrack Hong Kong, China Watchdog has Cathay Staff 'Walking on Eggshells.'" *Reuters*. October 3.

Frieden, Jeffry. 2006. *Global Capitalism: Its Fall and Rise in the Twentieth Century*. New York: W.W. Norton & Company.

Frye, Timothy. 2010. *Building States and Markets After Communism: The Perils of Polarized Democracy*. New York: Cambridge University Press.

Fuchs, Andreas, and Marina Rudyak. 2019. "The Motives of China's Foreign Aid," in Ka Zeng (ed.) *Handbook of of the International Political Economy of China*. Cheltenham: Edward Elgar. Ch. 23.

Funabashi, Yoichi and Barak Kushner. Eds. 2015. *Examining Japan's Lost Decades*. New York: Routledge.

Gallagher, Mary. 2005. *Contagious Capitalism: Globalization and the Politics of Labor in China*. Princeton: Princeton University Press.

Gangl, Manfred. 2016. "The Controversy over Frederick Pollock's State Capitalism." *History of the Human Sciences* 29(2): 23–41.

Gao, Simin. 2020. "Anti-'Grey Rhino': Prudential Regulation and Bank Resolution in China," in Douglas W. Arner, Wai Yee Wan, Gandrew Godwin, Wei Shen, and Evan Gibson (eds.), *Research Handbook on Asian Financial Law*. Cheltenham: Edward Elgar, 274–92.

Garcia-Herrero, Alicia. 2021. "What is Behind China's Dual Circulation Strategy?" *China Leadership Monitor* 69. https://ssrn.com/abstract=3927117.

Garnaut, Ross, Ligang Song, Yang Yao, and Xiaolu Wang. 2012. *Private Enterprise in China*. Sydney: ANU Press. www.jstor.org/stable/j.ctt24hdbj.17.

Gerschenkron, Alexander. 1962. *Economic Backwardness in Historical Perspective: A Book of Essays*. New York: Praeger: 5–30.

Gilley, Bruce. 2004. *China's Democratic Future: How it Will Happen and Where it Will Lead*. New York: Columbia University Press.

Goldstein, Avery. 2020. "China's Grand Strategy under Xi Jinping: Reassurance, Reform, and Resistance." *International Security* 45(1): 164–201.

Gourevitch, Peter. 1986. *Politics in Hard Times: Comparative Responses to International Economic Crises*. Ithaca, NY: Cornell University Press.

Graham, Edward, and David Marchick. 2006. *U.S. National Security and Foreign Direct Investment*. Washington, DC: Institute for International Economics.

Greif, Avner, and David D. Laitin. 2004. "A Theory of Endogenous Institutional Change." *American Political Science Review* 98(4): 633–52.

Greitens, Sheena. 2016. *Dictators and their Secret Police: Coercive Institutions and State Violence*. New York: Cambridge University Press.

Greitens, Sheena, Myunghee Lee, Emir Yacizi. 2020. "Counterterrorism and Preventive Repression: China's Changing Strategy in Xinjiang." *International Security* 44(3): 9–47.

Griffin, Roger. 1991. *The Nature of Fascism*. New York: St. Martin's Press.

Grigg Angus. 2019. "No Such Thing as a Private Company in China: FIRB." *Financial Review*. January 16. www.afr.com/policy/foreign-affairs/no-such-thing-as-a-private-company-in-china-firb-20190116-h1a4ut.

Gunder Frank, Andre. 1966. "The Development of Underdevelopment." *Monthly Review* 18(4) (September): 17–31.

Guo, Quanzhong. 2017. "Teshu guanli gu ruhe luodi" ["How to implement 'special management shares' in reality"]. *Zhongguo chuban chuanmei shangbao [China Publishing and Media Journal]*. Reprinted at www.sohu .com/a/200512650_481352.

Guthrie, Douglas. 1999. *Dragon in a Three-Piece Suit: The Emergence of Capitalism in China*. Princeton: Princeton University Press.

Guthrie, Douglas, Zhixing Xiao, and Junmin Wang. 2015. "Stability, Asset Management, and Gradual Change in China's Reform Economy," in Barry Naughton and Kellee S. Tsai (eds.) *State Capitalism, Institutional Adaptation, and the Chinese Miracle*. New York: Cambridge University Press, 75–101.

Hachem, Kinda. 2018. "Shadow Banking in China." *Annual Review of Financial Economics* 10(1): 287–308. https://doi.org/10.1146/annurev-finan cial-110217-023025.

Haggard, Stephan. 1989. "The East Asian NICs in Comparative Perspective." *The Annals of the American Academy of Political and Social Science* 505 (September): 129–41.

Haggard, Stephan. 1990. *Pathways from the Periphery: The Politics of Growth in the Newly-Industrializing Countries*. Ithaca, NY: Cornell University Press.

Haggard, Stephan. 2018. *Developmental States*. New York: Cambridge University Press.

Hall, Thomas W. and John Elliott. 1999. "Poland and Russia One Decade after Shock Therapy." *Journal of Economic Issues* 33(2) (June): 305–4.

Hancock, Tom. 2018. "China Nationalises Troubled Conglomerate Anbang." *Financial Times*. June 22. www.ft.com/content/279318d4-75fd-11e8-b326-75a27d27ea5f.

Hanemann, Thilo, and Mikko Huotari. 2018. "EU-China FDI: Working Towards Reciprocity in Investment Relations." *MERICS Papers on China*, 3. https://

merics.org/sites/default/files/2020-04/180723_MERICS-COFDI-Update_final_0.pdf.

Hanemann, Thilo, Mark Witzke, Charlie Vest, Lauren Dudley, and Ryan Featherstone. 2022. "Two Way Street – An Outbound Investment Screening Regime for the United States?" *Rhodium Group*. January 26. https://rhg.com/research/tws-outbound/.

Hall, Peter A. 2020. "The Electoral Politics of Growth Regimes." *Perspectives on Politics* 18(1) (March): 185–99.

Hall, Peter A., and David Soskice. 2001. *Varieties of Capitalism: The Institutional Foundations of Comparative Advantage*. Oxford: Oxford University Press.

He, Huifeng. 2017. "German Trade Body Warns Firms May Pull out of China over Communist Party Pressure." *South China Morning Post*. November 29. www.scmp.com/news/china/economy/article/2122104/german-trade-body-warns-firms-may-pull-out-china-over-communist.

He, Qing, and Xiaoyang Li. 2020. "The Failures of Peer-to-Peer Lending Platform Finance and Politics." *Journal of Corporate Finance* 66, 101852.

Heberer, Thomas, and Gunter Schubert. 2020. *Weapons of the Rich: Strategic Action of Private Entrepreneurs in Contemporary China*. Singapore: World Scientific Publishing.

Heilmann, Sebastian and Elizabeth J. Perry. Eds. 2011. *Mao's Invisible Hand: The Political Foundations of Adaptive Governance in China*. Harvard Contemporary China Series. Cambridge: Harvard University Press.

Heilmann, Sebastian, and Leah Shih. 2013. "The Rise of Industrial Policy in China, 1978–2012." *Harvard-Yenching Institute Working Paper Series* 17 (7): 1–24.

Hellman, Joel S. 1998. "Winners Take All: The Politics of Partial Reform in Postcommunist Transitions." *World Politics* 50(2) (January): 203–34.

Hellman, Joel S., Geraint Jones, and Daniel Kaufmann. 2003. "Seize the State, Seize the Day: State Capture and Influence in Transition Economies." *Journal of Comparative Economics* 31(4): 751–73.

Henning, Eyk. 2016. "U.S. Regulators Move to Stop Chinese Takeover of German Tech Firm Aixtron." *Wall Street Journal* (November 20), www.wsj.com/articles/u-s-regulators-move-to-stop-chinese-takeover-of-german-tech-firm-aixtron-1479549362.

Hinton, William. 1968. *Fanshen: A Documentary of Revolution in a Chinese Village*. New York: Vintage Press.

Holbig, Heike. 2018. "Whose New Normal? Framing the Economic Slowdown under Xi Jinping." *Journal of Chinese Political Science* 23: 341–63.

Hornby, Lucy, Sherry Fei Ju, and Louise Lucas. 2018. "China Cracks Down on Tech Credit Scoring." *Financial Times*. February 4. www.ft.com/content/f23e0cb2-07ec-11e8-9650-9c0ad2d7c5b5.

Hou, Yue. 2019. "The Private Sector: Challenges and Opportunities During Xi's Second Term." *China Leadership Monitor*. March 1. www.prcleader.org/hou.

Hsing, You-Tien. 2010. *The Great Urban Transformation: Politics of Land and Property in China*. Oxford: Oxford University Press.

Hsueh, Roselyn. 2011. *China's Regulatory State: A New Strategy for Globalization*. Ithaca, NY: Cornell University Press.

Huang, Dongya, and Minglu Chen. 2019. "Business Lobbying within the Party-State: Embedding Lobbying and Political Co-optation in China." *China Journal* 83. https://doi.org/10.1086/705933.

Huang, Jingyang, and Kellee S. Tsai. 2021. "Upgrading Big Brother: Strategic Adaptation in China's Security Industry." *Studies in Comparative International Development* 56 (October): 560–87.

Huang, Jingyang, and Kellee S. Tsai. 2022. "Securing Authoritarian Capitalism: The Political Economy of Surveillance in China." *China Journal* 88 (July): 1–27.

Huang, Philip C.C. 2011. "Chongqing: Equitable Development Driven by a Third Hand." *Modern China* 37(6): 569–622.

Huang, Tianlei, and Nicolas Véron. 2022. "The Private Sector Advances in China: The Evolving Ownership Structures of the Largest Companies in the Xi Jinping Era." Peterson Institute for International Economics (PIIE) Working Paper No. 22–3. Washington, DC: PIIE.

Huang, Yasheng. 2003. *Selling China: Foreign Direct Investment During the Reform Era*. New York: Cambridge University Press.

Huang, Yasheng. 2008. *Capitalism with Chinese Characteristics: Entrepreneurship and the Chinese State*. New York: Cambridge University Press.

Hufbauer, Gary Clyde, and Euijin Jung. 2020. "What's New in Economic Sanctions?" *European Economic Review* 130: 1–12. https://doi.org/10.1016/j.euroecorev.2020.103572.

Huntington, Samuel P. 1968. *Political Order in Changing Societies*. New Haven, CT: Yale University Press.

Hurst, William. 2009. *The Chinese Worker after Socialism*. Cambridge: Cambridge University Press.

Ikenberry G. John. 2008. "The Rise of China and the Future of the West, Can the Liberal System Survive?" *Foreign Affairs* (January/February).

Inkeles, Alex. 1966. *The Modernization of Man*. Cambridge, MA: Harvard University Press.

Inoue, Carlos, Sergio Lazzarini, and Aldo Musacchio. 2013. "Leviathan as a Minority Shareholder: Firm-Level Implications of State Equity Purchases." *Academy of Management Journal* 56(6): 1775–801.

James, C. L. R., Raya Dunayevskaya, and Grace Boggs. 1986 [1950]. *State Capitalism and World Revolution*. Chicago: Charles H. Kerr.

Jiang, Emily. 2019. "Burger King Faces Boycott in China After Calling Coronavirus the 'Wuhan Pneumonia' on Facebook." *Mail Online*. March 30.

Johnson, Chalmers. 1982. *MITI and the Japanese Miracle: The Growth of Industrial Policy, 1925–1975*. Stanford: Stanford University Press.

Johnson, Chalmers. 1995. *Japan: Who Governs? The Rise of the Developmental State*. New York: W. W. Norton.

Jones, Derek C., Cheng Li, and Ann L. Owen. 2003. "Growth and Regional Inequality in China during the Reform Era." *China Economic Review* 14(2): 186–200.

Kahler, Miles, and David A. Lake. 2013. *Politics in the New Hard Times: The Great Recession in Comparative Perspective*. Ithaca, NY: Cornell University Press.

Kelliher, Daniel. 1992. *Peasant Power in China; The Era of Rural Reform, 1979–1989*. New Haven, CT: Yale University Press.

Kerkvliet, Ben, Anita Chan, and Jonathan Unger. 1998. "Comparing the Chinese and Vietnam Reforms: An Introduction." *China Journal* 40 (July): 1–7.

Kinder, Tabby. 2021. "Jamie Dimon Apologizes Twice After Saying JPMorgan Will Outlast China's Communist Party." *Financial Times*. November 25.

Kornai, János. 1980. "The Dilemmas of a Socialist Economy: The Hungarian Experience." *Cambridge Journal of Economics* 4(2): 147–57.

Kornai, János. 2016. "The System Paradigm Revisited: Clarification and Additions in the Light of Experiences in the Post-Socialist Region." *Acta Oeconomica* 66(4): 547–96.

Koss, Daniel. 2021. "Party Building as Institutional Bricolage: Asserting Authority at the Business Frontier." *China Quarterly* 248 (November): 222–43.

Koty, Alexander Chipman. 2022. "How to Understand China's Common Prosperity Policy." *China Briefing*. March 21.

Kraus, Willy. 1991. *Private Business in China: Revival between Ideology and Pragmatism*. Honolulu: University of Hawaii Press.

Kroeber, Arthur. 2016. *China's Economy: What Everyone Needs to Know*. New York: Oxford University Press.

Kurlantzick, Joshua. 2016. *State Capitalism: How the Return of Statism is Transforming the World*. New York: Oxford University Press.

Lardy, Nicholas. 1994. *China in the World Economy*. Washington, DC: Institute for International Economics.

Lardy, Nicholas R. 1998. *China's Unfinished Economic Revolution*. Washington, DC: Brookings Institution Press.

Lardy, Nicholas. 2008. "Financial Repression in China." Peterson Institute for International Economics Working Paper No. PB08-8.

Lardy, Nicholas R. 2014. *Markets Over Mao: The Rise of Private Business in China*. Washington, DC: Peterson Institute for International Economics.

Lardy, Nicholas R. 2019. *The State Strikes Back: The End of Economic Reform in China?* Washington, DC: Peterson Institute for International Economics.

Lenin, Vladimir I. 2010 [1916]. *Imperialism: The Highest Stage of Capitalism*. New York: Penguin Classics.

Leutert, Wendy. 2018. "Firm Control: Governing the State-owned Economy under Xi Jinping." *China Perspectives* 1–2: 27–36.

Leutert, Wendy, and Sarah Eaton. 2021. "Deepening Not Departure: Xi Jinping's Governance of China's State-owned Economy." *China Quarterly* 248 (November): 200–21.

Lewis, Margaret K. 2021. "Criminalizing China." *Journal of Law and Criminology* 111(1): 145–225.

Li, Anthony H. F. 2017. "E-commerce and Taobao Villages." *China Perspectives* 3: 57–62.

Li, He. 2010. "Debating China's Economic Reform: New Leftists vs. Liberals." *Journal of Chinese Political Science* 15(10):1–23.

Li, Lianjiang, and Kevin O'Brien. 1999. "Selective Policy Implementation in Rural China." *Comparative Politics* 31(2): 167–86.

Liang, Fan. 2020. "COVID-19 and Health Code: How Digital Platforms Tackle the Pandemic in China." *Social Media + Society* 6(3) (July–September): 1–4.

Liang, Fan, Vishnupriya Das, Nadiya Kostyuk, and Muzammil M. Hussain. 2018. "Constructing a Data-Driven Society: China's Social Credit System as a State Surveillance Infrastructure." *Policy & Internet* 10(4): 415–53.

Liebknecht, Wilhelm. 1896. "Our Recent Congress." *Justice*. August 15: 4. www.marxists.org/archive/liebknecht-w/1896/08/our-congress.htm.

Lin, Justin Yifu, and Xiaobing Wang. 2021. "Dual Circulation: A New Structural Economics View of Development." *Journal of Chinese Economic and Business Studies* 20(4): 303–22. https://doi.org/10.1080/14765284.2021.1929793.

Lin, Li-Wen, and Curtis J. Milhaupt. 2013. "We Are the (National) Champions: Understanding the Mechanisms of State Capitalism in China." *Stanford Law Review* 65: 697–759.

Lin, Yi-min. 2017. *Dancing with the Devil: The Political Economy of Privatization in China*. Oxford: Oxford University Press.

Lindblom, Charles E. 1977. *Politics and Markets: The World's Political-Economic Systems*. New York: Basic Books.

Lipset, Seymour Martin. 1959. "Some Social Requisites of Democracy: Economic Development and Political Legitimacy." *American Political Science Review* 53(1): 69–105.

List, Friedrich. 1841. *The National System of Political Economy*. Wilmington, DE: Vernan Art and Science, Inc. http://oll.libertyfund.org/titles/list-the-national-system-of-political-economy.

Liu, Adam Y., Jean C. Oi, and Yi Zhang. 2022. "China's Local Government Debt: The Grand Bargain." *China Journal* 87(1) (January): 40–71.

Liu, Lizhi, and Barry R. Weingast. 2018. "Taobao, Federalism, and the Emergence of Law, Chinese Style." *Minnesota Law Review* 102(4): 1563–90.

Liu, Mingtang, and Kellee S. Tsai. 2021. "Structural Power, Hegemony, and State Capitalism: Limits to China's Relative Economic Power." *Politics & Society* 49(2) (June): 235–67.

Looney, Kristen. 2020. *Mobilizing for Development: The Modernization of Rural East Asia*. Ithaca, NY: Cornell University Press.

Looney, Kristen, and Meg Rithmire. 2017. "China's Gamble on Modernizing through Urbanization." *Current History* (September): 203–09.

Lowi, Theodore. 1979. *The End of Liberalism: The Second Republic of the United States*. Second edition. New York: W.W. Norton and Co.

Lü, Xiaobo. 2000. "Booty Socialism, Bureau-preneurs, and the State in Transition: Organizational Corruption in China." *Comparative Politics* 32 (3) (April): 273–94.

Lü, Xiaobo, and Pierre F. Landry. 2014. "Show Me the Money: Interjurisdiction Political Competition and Fiscal Extraction in China." *American Political Science Review* 108(3): 706–22.

Lutz, Catherine. 2018. "FBI Director Christopher Wray Wants to Talk about More than Russia." Aspen Institute. July 20. www.aspeninstitute.org/blog-posts/fbi-director-christopher-wray-wants-talk-about-more-than-russia/.

Lyttelton, Adrian. 1973. *The Seizure of Power: Fascism in Italy 1919–1929*. London: Weidenfield and Nicolson.

Mann, Michael. 1984. "The Autonomous Power of the State." *European Journal of Sociology* 25(2): 185–213.

Marcuse, Herbert. 1998 [1942]. "State and Individual Under National Socialism," in Douglas Kellner (ed.), *Technology, War and Fascism: Collected Papers of Herbert Marcuse*, Volume 1. London: Routledge, 67–88.

McArdle, Mairead. 2020. "Leading Scientific Journal *Nature* Apologizes for 'Associating' Coronavirus with China." *National Review.* April 9. https://www.nationalreview.com/news/leading-scientific-journal-nature-apologizes-for-associating-coronavirus-with-china/.

McMillan, John, and Barry Naughton. 1992. "How to Reform a Planned Economy: Lessons from China." *Oxford Review of Economic Policy* 8(1): 130–43.

McNally, Christopher. 2012. "Sino-Capitalism: China's Re-emergence and the International Political Economy." *World Politics* 64(4): 741–76.

McNamara, Kathleen, and Abraham Newman. 2020. "The Big Reveal: COVID-19 and Globalization's Great Transformations. *International Organization* 74(S1): E59–E77.

Meyer, Marshall W., and Changqi Wu. 2014. "Making Ownership Matter: Prospects for China's Mixed Ownership Economy." Paulson Policy Memorandum. Chicago: Paulson Institute. https://macropolo.org/wp-content/uploads/2017/05/PPM_Making-Ownership-Matter_Meyer-and-Wu_English_R.pdf.

Milhaupt, Curtis J. 2020. "The State as Owner – China's Experience." *Oxford Review of Economic Policy* 36(2): 362–79.

Minzner, Carl. 2018. *End of an Era: How China's Authoritarian Revival is Undermining its Rise.* New York: Oxford University Press.

Moore, Barrington. 1966. *Social Origins of Dictatorship and Democracy: Lord and Peasant in the Making of the Modern World.* Boston: Beacon Press.

Morgan, Pippa. 2019. "Can China's Economic Statecraft Win Soft Power in Africa? Unpacking Trade, Investment and Aid." *Journal of Chinese Political Science* 24(3): 387–409. https://doi.org/10.1007/s11366-018-09592-w.

Mozur, Paul, and Jack Ewing. 2016. "Rush of Chinese Investment in Europe's High-Tech Firms Is Raising Eyebrows." *New York Times.* September 16. www.nytimes.com/2016/09/17/business/dealbook/china-germany-takeover-merger-technology.html.

Murrell, Peter. 1993. "What is Shock Therapy? What Did it Do to Poland and Russia?" *Post-Soviet Affairs* 9(2): 111–40.

Nahm, Jonas, and Edward Steinfeld. 2014. "Scale-Up Nation: China's Specialization in Innovative Manufacturing." *World Development.* 54: 288–300.

National People's Congress. 2007. "The Property Law of the People's Republic of China" ["Zhonghua Renmin Gongheguo wuquanfa"]. March 16. https://web.archive.org/web/20190615114414/http://www.npc.gov.cn/englishnpc/Law/2009-02/20/content_1471118.htm.

National People's Congress. 2020. "Civil Code of the People's Republic of China" ["Zhonghua Renmin Gongheguo minfadian"]. May 28. www.chinalawtranslate.com/en/civilcode/.

National People's Congress. 2021. "Anti-Foreign Sanctions Law of the PRC." June 10.www.npc.gov.cn/npc/c30834/202106/d4a714d5813c4ad2ac54a5f0f78a5270.shtml.

Nathan, Andrew J. 2003. "China's Changing of the Guard: Authoritarian Resilience." *Journal of Democracy* 14(1) (January): 6–17.

Naughton, Barry. 2007. *The Chinese Economy: Transitions and Growth.* Cambridge, MA: MIT Press.

Naughton, Barry. 2014. "After the Third Plenum: Economic Reform Revival Moves toward Implementation." *China Leadership Monitor* 43. March 14.

Naughton, Barry. 2017. "Is China Socialist?" *Journal of Economic Perspectives* 31(1) (Winter): 3–24.

Naughton, Barry. 2018. *The Chinese Economy: Adaptation and Growth*, 2nd ed. Cambridge, MA: MIT Press.

Naughton, Barry. 2019a. "Financialisation of the State Sector in China," in Yongnian, Zheng, and Sarah Y. Tong (eds.), *China's Economic Modernization and Structural Changes: Essays in Honour of John Wong.* Singapore: World Scientific, 167–85.

Naughton, Barry. 2019b. "China's Domestic Economy: From 'Enlivening' to 'Steerage'," in Jacques deLisle and Avery Goldstein (eds.), *To Get Rich is Glorious: Challenges Facing China's Economic Reform and Opening at Forty.* Washington, DC: Brookings Press, 29–54.

Naughton, Barry. 2021. *The Rise of China's Industrial Policy, 1978–2020.* Mexico: Universidad Nacional Autónomica de México, Facultad de Economía.

Naughton, Barry, and Kellee S. Tsai. 2015. "State Capitalism and the Chinese Economic Miracle," in Barry Naughton and Kellee S. Tsai (eds.), *State Capitalism, Institutional Adaptation, and the Chinese Miracle.* New York: Cambridge University Press, 1–24.

Nee, Victor, and Sonja Opper. 2012. *Capitalism from Below: Markets and Institutional Change in China.* Cambridge, MA: Harvard University Press.

Nelson, Richard R. 1993. *National Innovation Systems: A Comparative Analysis.* New York: Oxford University Press.

Nelson, Richard R., and Sidney G. Winter. 1982. *An Evolutionary Theory of Economic Change*. Cambridge, MA: Harvard University Press.

Niewenhuis, Lucas. 2019. "All the International Brands that have Apologized to China." Supchina.com. October 26. https://signal.supchina.com/all-the-inter national-brands-that-have-apologized-to-china/.

Norris, William. 2016. *China's Economic Statecraft: Commercial Actors, Grand Strategy, and State Control*. Ithaca, NY: Cornell University Press.

OECD. 2019. "Measuring Distortions in International Markets: The Semiconductor Value Chain." *OECD Trade Policy Papers*, No. 234.

Oi, Jean C. 1999. *Rural China Takes Off: Institutional Foundations of Economic Reforms*. Berkeley: University of California Press.

Oi, Jean C., and Andrew Walder, eds. 1999. *Property Rights and Economic Reform in China*. Stanford: Stanford University Press.

Olson, Mancur. 1982. *The Rise and Decline of Nations: Economic Growth, Stagflation, and Social Rigidities*. New Haven, CT: Yale University Press.

Ong, Lynette. 2014. "State-led Urbanization in China: Skyscrapers, Land Revenue and 'Concentrated Villages.'" *China Quarterly* 217: 162–79.

Ong, Lynette. 2022. *Outsourcing Repression: Everyday State Power in Contemporary China*. New York: Oxford University Press.

Patey, Luke. 2020. *How China Loses: The Pushback against Chinese Global Ambitions*. Oxford: Oxford University Press.

Paxton, Robert O. 2004. *The Anatomy of Fascism*. New York: Alfred A. Knopf.

Pearson, Margaret M. 1992. *Joint Ventures in the People's Republic of China: The Control of Foreign Direct Investment under Socialism*. Princeton: Princeton University Press.

Pearson, Margaret. 2005. "The Business of Governing Business in China: Institutions and Norms of the Emerging Regulatory State." *World Politics* 57(2): 296–322.

Pearson, Margaret M. 2015. "State-Owned Business and Party-State Regulation in China's Modern Political Economy," in Barry Naughton and Kellee S. Tsai (eds.), *State Capitalism, Institutional Adaptation, and the Chinese Miracle*. New York: Cambridge University Press, 27–45.

Pearson, Margaret M. 2019. "Local Government and Firm Innovation: China's Clean Energy Sector," in Loren Brandt and Thomas Rawski (eds.), *Policy, Regulation and Innovation in Chinese Industry*. New York: Cambridge University Press, 96–133.

Pearson, Margaret, and Tianbiao Zhu. 2013. "Globalization and the Role of the State." *Review of International Political Economy* 20:6 (December): 1215–43.

Pearson, Margaret, Meg Rithmire, and Kellee S. Tsai. 2021. "Party-State Capitalism in China." *Current History* 120(827) (September): 207–13.

Pearson, Margaret, Meg Rithmire, and Kellee S. Tsai. 2022. "China's Political Economy and International Backlash: From Interdependence to Security Dilemma Dynamics." *International Security* 47(2) (Fall): 135–76.

Pei, Minxin. 2006. *China's Trapped Transition: The Limits of Developmental Autocracy*. Cambridge, MA: Harvard University Press.

Pei, Minxin. 2016. *China's Crony Capitalism: The Dynamics of Regime Decay*. Cambridge, MA: Harvard University Press.

Pempel, T. J. 2021. *A Region of Regimes: Prosperity and Plunder in the Asia-Pacific*. Ithaca, NY: Cornell University Press.

People's Republic of China (PRC). 2015. National Security Law of the People's Republic of China. July 1. English translation: https://govt.chinadaily.com.cn/s/201812/11/WS5c0f1b56498eefb3fe46e8c9/national-security-law-of-the-peoples-republic-of-china-2015-effective.html.

People's Republic of China (PRC). 2017. National Intelligence Law of the People's Republic of China. June 27. English translation: www.xinhuanet.com//english/2017-06/27/c_136398422.htm.

People's Republic of China (PRC) Central Government Portal. 2007. "Wen Jiabao: China Has the Conditions to Maintain Stable and Rapid Economic Development" [in Chinese]. March 16. www.gov.cn/wszb/zhibo20070316b/content_552718.htm.

People's Republic of China (PRC) Ministry of Industry and Information Technology. 2017. "Guiding Opinions of 16 Departments including the Ministry of Industry and Information Technology on Giving Full Play to the Role of Private Investment to Promote the Implementation of the Strategy of Manufacturing Power." No. 243. www.miit.gov.cn/n1146285/n1146352/n3054355/n3057527/n7407498/c7435073/content.html.

People's Republic of China (PRC) State Council. 2013. "Decision on Major Problems of Deepening Reform" [in Chinese]. November 15. www.gov.cn/jrzg/2013-11/15/content_2528179.htm.

People's Republic of China (PRC) State Council. 2015. "Guiding Opinions on Deepening Reform of State-Owned Enterprises" [in Chinese]. No. 22 Document. September 13. www.gov.cn/zhengce/2015-09/13/content_2930440.htm.

Perry, Elizabeth J. 2019. "Making Communism Work: Sinicizing a Soviet Governance Practice." *Comparative Studies in History and Society* 61(3): 535–62.

Perry, Elizabeth J. 2021. "Epilogue: China's (Re)volutionary Governance and the COVID-19 Crisis," in Szu-chien Hsu, Kellee S. Tsai, and Chun-chih

Chang (eds.), *Evolutionary Governance in China: State-Society Relations under Authoritarianism*. Cambridge, MA: Harvard Asia Center, 387–96.

Perry, Elizabeth J., and Li Xun. 1997. *Proletarian Power: Shanghai in the Cultural Revolution*. Boulder, CO: Westview Press.

Polanyi, Karl. 1957. *The Great Transformation*. New York: Rinehart.

Pollock, Fredrick. 1941. "State Capitalism: Its Possibilities and Limitations." *Studies in Philosophy and Social Science* 9(2): 200–25.

Polyakova, Alina, and Chris Meserole. 2019. "Exporting Digital Authoritarianism: The Russian and Chinese Models." Brookings Institution Democracy and Disorder Policy Brief. August. Washington, DC: Brooking Institution. www.brookings.edu/wp-content/uploads/2019/08/FP_20190827_digital_authoritarianism_polyakova_meserole.pdf.

Prasso, Sheridan. 2020. "Mao's 'Magic Weapon' Casts a Dark Spell on Hong Kong." *Bloomberg News*. June 18. www.bloombergquint.com/business week/china-s-united-front-pressures-support-for-hong-kong-laws.

PRC Supreme People's Court Network. 2015. "Supreme People's Court Cooperates with Sesame Credit Network to Punish Misconduct" [in Chinese]. December 20. www.court.gov.cn/zixun-xiangqing-16351.html.

President's Council of Advisors on Science and Technology. 2017. "Report to the President: Ensuring Long-Term U.S. Leadership in Semiconductors." https://obamawhitehouse.archives.gov/sites/default/files/microsites/ostp/PCAST/pcast_ensuring_long-term_us_leadership_in_semiconductors.pdf.

Przeworski, Adam. 2019. *Crises of Democracy*. Cambridge, MA: Cambridge University Press.

Przeworski, Adam, and Fernando Limongi. 1997. "Modernization: Theories and Facts." *World Politics* 49(2): 155–83.

Pye, Lucian. 1992. *The Spirit of Chinese Politics* [New Edition]. Cambridge, MA: Harvard University Press.

Qiushi. 2018. "Renqing 'guojia zibenzhuyi' wenti de zhenxiang" ["Recognize the truth about 'state capitalism'"]. *Qiushi* [Seeking Truth]. www.qstheory.cn/dukan/qs/2018-09/01/c_1123362691.htm.

Ratigan, Kerry. 2021. "Are Peruvians Enticed by the 'China Model'? Chinese Investment and Public Opinion in Peru." *Studies in Comparative International Development* 56(1) (March): 87–111.

Repnikova, Maria. 2022. *Chinese Soft Power*. New York: Cambridge University Press.

Rhodium China Investment Monitor (online tool). https://rhg.com/impact/china-investment-monitor/.

Rithmire, Meg. 2012. "The 'Chongqing Model' and the Future of China." HBS Case 713-028. December.

Rithmire, Meg. 2014. "China's 'New Regionalism': Subnational Analysis in Chinese Political Economy." *World Politics* 66(1) (January): 165–94.

Rithmire, Meg. 2015. *Land Bargains and Chinese Capitalism: The Politics of Property Rights under Reform*. New York: Cambridge University Press.

Rithmire, Meg. 2022. "Going Out or Opting Out? Capital, Political Vulnerability, and the State in China's Outward Direct Investment." *Comparative Politics* 54(3) (April): 477–99.

Rithmire, Meg, and Hao Chen. 2021. "The Emergence of Mafia-like Business Systems in China." *China Quarterly* 248(1): 1037–58.

Rithmire, Meg, and Courtney Han. 2021. "The Clean Network and the Future of Global Technology Competition." HBS Case 721-045. Cambridge, MA: Harvard Business School Publishing.

Rithmire, Meg, and Yihao Li. 2019. "Lattice Semiconductor and the Future of Chinese High-Tech Acquisitions in the United States." HBS Case 719-059. Cambridge, MA: Harvard Business School Publishing.

Rodrik, Dani, and Stefanie Stantcheva. 2021. "Fixing Capitalism's Good Jobs Problem." *Oxford Review of Economic Policy* 37(4): 824–37.

Rodrik, Dani, Arvind Subramanian, and Francesco Trebbi. 2004. "Institutions Rule: The Primacy of Institutions over Geography and Integration In Economic Development." *Journal of Economic Growth* 9(2): 131–65.

Rosen, Dan. 2021. "China's Economic Reckoning: The Price of Failed Reforms." *Foreign Affairs*. July/August. www.foreignaffairs.com/articles/china/2021-06-22/chinas-economic-reckoning.

Rudd, Kevin. 2022. "The Return of Red China: Xi Jinping Brings Back Marxism." *Foreign Affairs*. November 9. www.foreignaffairs.com/china/return-red-china.

Ruggie, John G. 1982. "International Regimes, Transactions, and Change: Embedded Liberalism in the Postwar Economic Order." *International Organization* 36(2): 379–415.

Sachs, Jeffrey. D. 1993. *Poland's Jump to the Market Economy*. Cambridge, MA: MIT Press.

Sachs, Jeffrey, and Wing Thye Woo. 1994. "Structural Factors in the Economic Reforms of China, Eastern Europe, and the Former Soviet Union." *Economic Policy* 9(18) (April): 101–45.

Segal, Adam. 2003. *Digital Dragons: High Technology Enterprises in China*. Ithaca, NY: Cornell University Press.

Sevastopulo, Demetri and Andrew Edgecliffe-Johnson. 2021. "Western Brands Caught Between US and China over Human Rights." *Financial Times*. April 2.

Schumpeter, Joseph. 1911. *The Theory of Economic Development: An Inquiry into Profits, Capital, Credit, Interest, and the Business Cycle.* Cambridge, MA: Harvard University Press.

Shen, Xiaoxiao, and Kellee S. Tsai. 2016. "Institutional Adaptability in China: Local Developmental Models under Changing Economic Conditions." *World Development* 87: 107–27.

Shi, Tianjian. 1997. *Political Participation in Beijing.* Cambridge, MA: Harvard University Press.

Shih, Gerry. 2019. "Chinese State TV Cancels Broadcasts of NBA Preseason Games and Sponsors Drop Out in Dispute over Hong Kong Comments." *Washington Post*. October 8. www.washingtonpost.com/world/asia_pacific/chinese-state-tv-cancels-broadcasts-of-nba-preseason-games-and-sponsors-drop-out-in-dispute-over-hong-kong-comments/2019/10/08/28f9dfd4-e9b8-11e9-bafb-da248f8d5734_story.html.

Shih, Victor. 2007. "Partial Reform Equilibrium, Chinese Style: Political Incentives and Reform Stagnation in Chinese Financial Policies." *Comparative Political Studies* 40(10): 1238–62.

Shih, Victor, Christopher Adolph, and Mingxing Liu. 2012. "Getting Ahead in the Communist Party: Explaining the Advancement of Central Committee Members in China." *American Political Science Review* 106(1): 116–87.

Shirk, Susan. 1993. *The Political Logic of Economic Reform.* Berkeley: University of California Press.

Shleifer, Andrei, and Robert Vishny. 1998. *The Grabbing Hand: Government Pathologies and Their Cures.* Cambridge, MA: Harvard University Press.

Shue, Vivienne. 1988. *The Reach of the State: Sketches of the Chinese Body Politic.* Stanford: Stanford University Press.

Slobodian, Quinn. 2020. "The World to Come: The Cycles of History." *The New Statesman*. August 26. www.newstatesman.com/world/2020/08/world-come-cycles-history.

Smith, Adam. 2002 [1776]. *The Wealth of Nations.* Oxford, England: Bibliomania.com Ltd.

Solinger, Dorothy J. 1987. *Chinese Business Under Socialism: The Politics of Domestic Commerce, 1984–1980.* Berkeley: University of California Press.

Solinger, Dorothy J. 1999. *Contesting Citizenship in Urban China: Peasant Migrants, the State, and the Logic of the Market.* Berkeley: University of California Press.

Sperber, Nathan. 2019. "The Many Lives of State Capitalism: From Classical Marxism to Free-market Advocacy." *History of the Human Sciences* 32(3): 100–24.

Standing Committee of the National People's Congress. 2015. "Counter-Terrorism Law of the People's Republic of China." Via China Law Translate. www.chinalawtranslate.com/en/counter-terrorism-law-2015/.

Stark, David. 1992. "Path Dependence and Privatization Strategies in East Central Europe." *East European Politics and Societies* 6(1) (Winter): 17–54.

Stern, Rachel E., and Jonathan Hassid. 2012. "Amplifying Silence: Uncertainty and Control Parables in Contemporary China." *Comparative Political Studies* 45(10): 1230–54.

Stevenson, Alexandra. 2020. "China Expels 3 Wall Street Journal Reporters as Media Relations Sour." *Wall Street Journal*. February 19.

Streeck, Wolfgang. 2014. "How Will Capitalism End?" *New Left Review* 87: 35–64.

Stuttaford, Andrew. 2022. "Fascism with Chinese Characeristics." *CapitalMatters* (February 1). www.nationalreview.com/corner/fascism-with-chinese-character istics/.

Sutherland, Dylan, and Lutao Ning. 2015. "The Emergence and Evolution of Chinese Business Groups: Are Pyramidal Groups Forming?" in Barry Naughton and Kellee S. Tsai (eds.), *State Capitalism, Institutional Adaptation, and the Chinese Miracle*. New York: Cambridge University Press, 102–53.

Tan, Yeling. 2020. "Disaggregating 'China, Inc.': The Hierarchical Politics of WTO Entry." *Comparative Political Studies* 53(13): 2118–52.

Tan, Yeling. 2021. *State Strategies under Global Rules: Chinese Industrial Policy in the WTO Era*. Ithaca, NY: Cornell University Press.

Tanner, Murray Scot. 2017. "Beijing's New National Intelligence Law: From Defense to Offense." *Lawfare*, July 20. www.lawfareblog.com/beiiings-new-national-intelligence-law-defense-offense.

Thelen, Kathleen. 2012. "Varieties of Capitalism: Trajectories of Liberalization and the New Politics of Social Solidarity." *Annual Review of Political Science* 15 (June): 137–59.

Thiessen, Marc A. 2022. "Opinion: Enes Freedom Was Cut for Exposing How U.S. Corporations Became Foreign Agents of Communist China." *Washington Post*. February 15. www.washingtonpost.com/opinions/2022/02/15/enes-kanter-freedom-nba-china-rockets/.

Tracy, Mark, Edward Wong, and Lara Jakes. 2020. "China Announces That It Will Expel American Journalists." *New York Times* (March 17).

Truex, Rory. 2016. *Making Autocracy Work: Representation and Responsiveness in Modern China*. Cambridge: Cambridge, University Press.

Tsai, Kellee S. 2002. *Back-Alley Banking: Private Entrepreneurs in China*. Ithaca, NY: Cornell University Press.

Tsai, Kellee S. 2006. "Adaptive Informal Institutions and Endogenous Institutional Change in China." *World Politics* 59(1): 116–41.

Tsai, Kellee S. 2007. *Capitalism without Democracy: The Private Sector in Contemporary China*. Ithaca, NY: Cornell University Press.

Tsai, Kellee S. 2017. "When Shadow Banking Can Be Productive: Financing Small and Medium Enterprises in China." *Journal of Development Studies* 53 (12): 2005–28.

Tsai, Kellee S. 2021. "Evolutionary Governance in China: State-Society Relations under Authoritarianism," in Szu-chien Hsu, Kellee S. Tsai, and Chun-chih Chang (eds.), *Evolutionary Governance in China: State-Society Relations under Authoritarianism*. Cambridge, MA: Harvard Asia Center, Harvard University Press, 3–37.

Tsai, Wen-Hsuan, Hsin-Hsien Wang, and Ruihua Lin. 2021. "Hobbling Big Brother: Top-Level Design and Local Discretion in China's Social Credit System." *China Journal* 86 (July): 1–20.

UNCTAD. Various years. *World Investment Report*. New York: United Nations.

US Congress. 2021. "United States Innovation and Competition Act of 2021." Library of Congress. 8 June, S.1260 – 117th Congress (2021–22). www .congress.gov/bill/117th-congress/senate-bill/1260.

US Department of the Treasury. 2018. "Provisions Pertaining to Certain Investments in the United States by Foreign Persons." *Federal Register* 83 (197) (October 11). https://home.treasury.gov/system/files/206/FR-2018-22187_1786944.pdf.

US House Intelligence Committee. 2012. "The House Intelligence Investigative Report on the U.S. National Security Issues Posed by Chinese Telecommunications Companies Huawei and ZTE." October 8. https://repub licans-intelligence.house.gov/sites/intelligence.house.gov/files/documents/huawei-zte%20investigative%20report%20(final).pdf.

Vinci, Anthony. 2020. "How to Stop China from Imposing Its Values." *The Atlantic*. August 2. www.theatlantic.com/ideas/archive/2020/08/like-nato-but-for-economics/614332/.

Vogel, Steven K. 2018. *Marketcraft: How Governments Make Markets Work*. New York: Oxford University Press.

Wade, Robert. 1990. *Governing the Market: Economic Theory and the Role of Government in East Asian Industrialization*. Princeton: Princeton University Press.

Walder, Andrew. 1986. *Communist Neo-Traditionalism: Work and Authority in Chinese Industry.* Berkeley: University of California Press.

Wallace, Jeremy. 2014. *Cities and Stability: Urbanization, Redistribution, and Regime Survival in China.* New York: Oxford University Press.

Wang, Feng. 2008. *Boundaries and Categories: Rising Inequality in Post-Socialist Urban China.* Stanford: Stanford University Press.

Wang, Q. Edward. 2009. "Modernization Theory in/of China." *Chinese Studies in History* 43(1) (Fall): 3–6.

Wang, Shujuan and Tianming Lan. 2019. "1400 duowan renci shenxian 'laolai' de beihou" ["Over 14 million people are 'dishonest persons'"]. *Xinhuanet.com.* November 12. http://m.xinhuanet.com/2019-11/12/c_1125223915.htm.

Wang, Xiaonan, Margaret M. Pearson, and John F. McCauley. 2022. "Foreign Direct Investment, Unmet Expectations, and the Prospects of Political Leaders: Evidence from Chinese Investment in Africa." *Journal of Politics* 84(3) (July).

Wang, Yingyao. 2015. "The Rise of the 'Shareholding State': Financialization of Economic Management in China." *Socio-Economic Review* 13(3): 603–25.

Wang, Yuhua. 2017. "Betting on a Princeling." *Studies in Comparative and International Development* 52 (4): 395–415.

Wang, Yuhua, and Carl Minzner. 2015. "The Rise of the Chinese Security State." *China Quarterly* 222: 339–59.

Weber, Isabella M. 2021. *How China Escaped Shock Therapy: The Market Reform Debate.* London: Routledge.

Weber, Max. 1958. *The Protestant Ethic and the Spirit of Capitalism.* New York: Scribner.

Wedeman, Andrew. 2003. *From Mao to Market: Rent Seeking, Local Protectionism, and Marketization in China.* New York: Cambridge University Press.

Wedeman, Andrew. 2012. *Double Paradox: Rapid Growth and Rising Corruption in China.* Ithaca, NY: Cornell University Press.

Weiss, Linda. *America, Inc.? Innovation and Enterprise in the National Security State.* Ithaca, NY: Cornell University Press. 2014.

Whiting, Susan. 2001. *Power and Wealth in Rural China: The Political Economy of Institutional Change.* Cambridge: Cambridge University Press.

Winters, Jeffrey. 2011. *Oligarchy.* Cambridge: Cambridge University Press.

Witt, Michael A., and Gordon Redding, eds. 2014. *The Oxford Handbook of Asian Business Systems.* Oxford: Oxford University Press.

Wong, Chun Han, and Eva Dou. 2017. "New Partner of Foreign Enterprises in China: Communist Party of China." *Wall Street Journal.* October 31. https://cn.wsj.com/articles/CT-BGH-20171030121119.

Woo, Wing Thye. 1999. "The Real Reasons for China's Growth." *The China Journal* 41 (January): 115–37.

Woo-Cumings, Meredith, ed. 1999. *The Developmental State.* Ithaca, NY: Cornell University Press.

World Bank. 1993. *The East Asian Growth Miracle: Economic Growth and Public Policy.* A World Bank Policy Research Report. New York: Oxford University Press.

Xiao, Qiang. 2019. "The Road to Digital Unfreedom: President Xi's Surveillance State." *Journal of Democracy* 30(1) (January): 53–67.

Xi, Jinping. 2017. "Secure a Decisive Victory in Building a Moderately Prosperous Society in All Respects and Strive for the Great Success of Socialism with Chinese Characteristics for a New Era." Speech delivered at the 19th National Congress of the Communist Party of China. October 18. www.xinhuanet.com/english/download/Xi_Jinping's_report_at_19th_CPC_National_Congress.pdf.

Xi Jinping. 2018a. "Speech on the 40th Anniversary of Reform and Opening." December 18. Partial translation: https://chinamediaproject.org/2018/12/18/reading-xis-reform-anniversary-speech/.

Xi, Jinping. 2018b. "Acutely Grasp the Historical Opportunity of Informationization Development; Move Forward the Construction of a Cyber Superpower Through Indigenous Innovation." Speech at the National Cybersecurity and Informationization Work Conference. April 20, Beijing. Rogier Creemers, Paul Triolo, and Graham Webster, translators. www.newamerica.org/cybersecurity-initiative/digichina/blog/translation-xi-jinpings-april-20-speech-national-cybersecurity-and-informatization-work-conference/.

Xi, Jinping. 2022. "Xi Jinping's Report at the 20th National Congress of the Chinese Communist Party." October 16. http://cpc.people.com.cn/20th/n1/2022/1026/c448334-32551867.html.

Xie, Yanmei. 2017. "China Unicom's Mixed-Ownership Mixup." *Gavekal Dragonomics.* August 25. www.gavekal.com.

Xinhua. 2013. "Market to Play 'Decisive' Role in Allocating Resources." November 12. www.china.org.cn/china/third_plenary_session/2013-11/12/content_30577689.htm.

Xinhua News Agency Wire. 2014. "Counter-Espionage Law of the PRC." Via China Law Translate, November 1. www.chinalawtranslate.com/en/anti-espionage/.

Xu, Xu. 2021. "To Repress or to Co-opt? Authoritarian Control in the Age of Digital Surveillance." *American Journal of Political Science* 65 (2): 309–25. https://doi.org/10.1111/ajps.12514.

Xue, Qing. 2017. "Country Garden: Taking Targeted Measures in Poverty Alleviation." *Nanfang zhoumo*. August 10. www.infzm.com/content/126591.

Yan, Xiaojun, and Jie Huang. 2017. "Navigating Unknown Waters: The Chinese Communist Party's New Presence in the Private Sector." *The China Review* 17(2): 37–63.

Yang, Dali. 1996. *Calamity and Reform in China: State, Rural Society, and Institutional Reform since the Great Leap Famine*. Stanford: Stanford University Press.

Yang, Dali. 2004. *Remaking the Chinese Leviathan: Market Transition and the Politics of Governance in China*. Stanford, CA: Stanford University Press.

Zeng, Julie, and Kellee S. Tsai. 2011. "The Local Politics of Restructuring State-Owned Enterprises in China," in Jean C. Oi, ed. *Going Private in China: The Politics of Corporate Restructuring and System Reform*. Stanford: Walter H. Shorenstein Asia-Pacific Research Center.

Zhai, Keith. 2021. "China Steps Up Direct Involvement in Internet-Content Firms." *Wall Street Journal*. August 17.

Zhang, Qi and Mingxing Liu. 2019. *Revolutionary Legacy, Power Structure, and Grassroots Capitalism under the Red Flag in China*. New York: Cambridge University Press.

Zhang, Xianchu. 2019. "Integration of CCP Leadership with Corporate Governance: Leading Role or Dismemberment?" *China Perspectives* 2019–1. https://journals.openedition.org/chinaperspectives/8770.

Zhao, Yanan. 2021. "Electronics Industry Comments: The Investment in the Second Phase of the Big Fund is Accelerating, and Semiconductor Equipment and Materials are Expected to Benefit First." *Guorong Securities*. November 11. https://data.eastmoney.com/report/zw_industry.jshtml?infocode=AP202111111528404639.

Zitelmann, Rainer. 2019. "State Capitalism: No, The Private Sector was and is the Main Driver of China's Economic Growth." *Forbes*. September 30.

Zweig, David. 2002. *Internationalizing China: Domestic Interests and Global Linkages*. Ithaca, NY: Cornell University Press.

Cambridge Elements ⹅

Politics and Society in East Asia

Erin Aeran Chung

Johns Hopkins University

Erin Aeran Chung is the Charles D. Miller Professor of East Asian Politics in the Department of Political Science at the Johns Hopkins University. She specializes in East Asian political economy, migration and citizenship, and comparative racial politics. She is the author of *Immigration and Citizenship in Japan* (Cambridge, 2010, 2014; Japanese translation, Akashi Shoten, 2012) and *Immigrant Incorporation in East Asian Democracies* (Cambridge, 2020). Her research has been supported by grants from the Academy of Korean Studies, the Japan Foundation, the Japan Foundation Center for Global Partnership, the Social Science Research Council, and the American Council of Learned Societies.

Mary Alice Haddad

Wesleyan University

Mary Alice Haddad is the John E. Andrus Professor of Government, East Asian Studies, and Environmental Studies at Wesleyan University. Her research focuses on democracy, civil society, and environmental politics in East Asia as well as city diplomacy around the globe. A Fulbright and Harvard Academy scholar, Haddad is author of *Effective Advocacy: Lessons from East Asia's Environmentalists* (MIT, 2021), *Building Democracy in Japan* (Cambridge, 2012), and *Politics and Volunteering in Japan* (Cambridge, 2007), and co-editor of *Greening East Asia* (University of Washington, 2021), and *NIMBY is Beautiful* (Berghahn Books, 2015). She has published in journals such as *Comparative Political Studies, Democratization, Journal of Asian Studies*, and *Nonprofit and Voluntary Sector Quarterly*, with writing for the public appearing in the *Asahi Shimbun*, the *Hartford Courant*, and the *South China Morning Post*.

Benjamin L. Read

University of California, Santa Cruz

Benjamin L. Read is a professor of Politics at the University of California, Santa Cruz. His research has focused on local politics in China and Taiwan, and he also writes about issues and techniques in comparison and field research. He is author of *Roots of the State: Neighborhood Organization and Social Networks in Beijing and Taipei* (Stanford, 2012), coauthor of *Field Research in Political Science: Practices and Principles* (Cambridge, 2015), and co-editor of *Local Organizations and Urban Governance in East and Southeast Asia: Straddling State and Society* (Routledge, 2009). His work has appeared in journals such as *Comparative Political Studies, Comparative Politics, the Journal of Conflict Resolution, the China Journal, the China Quarterly*, and *the Washington Quarterly*, as well as several edited books.

About the Series

The Cambridge Elements series on Politics and Society in East Asia offers original, multidisciplinary contributions on enduring and emerging issues in the dynamic region of East Asia by leading scholars in the field. Suitable for general readers and specialists alike, these short, peer-reviewed volumes examine common challenges and patterns within the region while identifying key differences between countries. The series consists of two types of contributions: 1) authoritative field surveys of established concepts and themes that offer roadmaps for further research; and 2) new research on emerging issues that challenge conventional understandings of East Asian politics and society. Whether focusing on an individual country or spanning the region, the contributions in this series connect regional trends with points of theoretical debate in the social sciences and will stimulate productive interchanges among students, researchers, and practitioners alike.

Cambridge Elements ≡

Politics and Society in East Asia

Printed in the USA
CPSIA information can be obtained
at www.ICGtesting.com
LVHW021240240823
756042LV00001B/81